# Why do I need a vocal coach?

## Stories, tips and hacks from the studio of a voice expert

JEREMY FISHER

# TESTIMONIALS

THE book to have on your shelf if you're coaching in 2020. This book is brilliant! Jam-packed with wit and wisdom. I felt it was really personal, honest and open. A fantastic practical yet entertaining toolkit for voice practitioners everywhere.
*Carrie Garrett SLT, singing teacher, voice rehabilitation coach*

Every performer should have this printed and annotated at the back of their rep folder! It's funny, full of insightful information and absolutely worth reading! As an MD I found myself reading it many times from the point of a performer, a vocal coach, an MD. I found something new every time I read it, and saw a lot of the points from multiple perspectives, which was extremely helpful!
*Connagh Tonkinson MD, Vocal Coach, Arranger*

Shot through with characteristic wit and generosity, and written in Jeremy's sharp-shooting prose, this is a great read, full of thoughtful, proven advice for vocalists – as well as coaches, teachers and (collaborative) pianists. Vocal Process are not shy in sharing their knowledge and this book represents a fleetful of treasure. There are industry hacks (just what does '16-bars' really mean?); tips on coping with audition pianists from hell (every singer has at least several of those in their past); and exercises for all manner of vocal techniques.

If this book had been available to me as a graduate it would have saved a world of heartache. Now, fifteen years later and with a career as a vocal and communications coach, I know I'll be returning to it time and again for gems of ideas and encouragement.
*Sophie Scott MA Cantab, Communications and Vocal Coach*

Jeremy is a hugely knowledgeable vocal practitioner and this book gives an insight into his praxis and process. This book is filled with tips and guidance for everything from approaches to operatic arias to accompanying yourself in the hotel bar, and Jeremy's convivial spirit, effervescent energy and humour are evident throughout.
*Clare Chandler MT singer, director, writer*

Jeremy's book manages to cover so much without ever making it feel hard work or dense. What I think sets it apart from many books offering advice in voice and singing production is the real life scenarios used to explain how a technique or piece of advice works with a client/student as opposed to just theoretical application.

This book will be an asset to any student singing in all styles and genres as well as teachers and coaches looking for fresh new approaches to their sessions, and as both a performer and teacher myself I found it informative from both perspectives.

From song choices to mindset, Jeremy delves into all areas of performance with humour and experience making you feel like you're in good hands reading this book.
*Richard Kent, actor singer with Phantom of the Opera (London West End)*

A fascinating insight into the role of the vocal coach, Fisher is generous in imparting a level of wisdom that can only be gained from decades of experience. He has developed a methodical approach to audition preparation and repertoire, which compliments *Successful Singing Auditions* (co-written with Dr Gillyanne Kayes) with further real-life examples, but never loses sight of the individual needs of the singer. His passion for collaboration is clear alongside an understanding of the broadest spectrum of musical styles. A thorough and nuanced guide, this is an essential read for any professional singer, singing teacher or vocal coach.
*Helen Power, MT and cabaret singer*

Right from the start I was in the room with Jeremy, a fly on the wall at one of his sessions. The style is anecdotal and conversational, with just the right balance of serious advice and humour, so true to how Jeremy presents in person. There are so many wide-ranging examples of vocal trouble-shooting and clearly explained solutions to such a range of performance issues, that this is a volume that a performer will re-visit again and again. Heartfelt, genuine and inspiring. It really made me think and reflect on my role, my life, and my tune. Thank you.
*Jessa Liversidge Singer and singing leader*

The book takes the reader through a very insightful journey of the modern vocal coach working in multi genre singing and the kinds of challenges you may see in the voice studio today. Full of useful hints and suggestions for whatever is your specialism from enthusiastic beginner to seasoned professional there is so much to gain from giving this a toot.
*Jacqui Podoski, singer, singing teacher, entrepreneur*

Every young musical theatre and opera singer needs to read Fisher's audition tips. This book was a delight to read, written in an engaging and conversational style. Fisher gives practical insights on a wide range of matters that concern singers of all backgrounds and specializations, while eschewing technical jargon in favor of the power to impart specialized knowledge to the general reader.
The tone of this book gave me the feeling that I was having a conversation with a friend who happened also to be an expert vocal coach delivering invaluable knowledge on diverse topics including acting technique, teaching children to match pitch, learning recitative, and maximizing the audition impact of songs you already know.

As an American classical singer, I especially appreciated the thorough description of the audition process in London's West End. While no word of advice could apply to every audition, this book contains powerful principles of successful auditioning concisely stated in a fun and approachable way. Fisher highlights key differences between styles of vocal music with practical techniques for singers wanting to cross over to other genres, a skill that is vital for singers in the twenty-first century.

I wish that this book had been in my library when I was learning my way around the stage!
*Marlayna Maynard, classical soprano, Director Vocal Studies, Radford University, VA*

First published 2020 by Canu Publishing, Alder Hollow, 10 West Wall,
Presteigne LD8 2BY
Canu Publishing is an imprint of Vocal Process Ltd


*British Library Cataloguing-in-Publication Data*
A catalogue record for this book is available from the British Library

*Library of Congress Cataloging-in-Publication Data*
A catalog record has been requested for this book

ISBN: **978-1-9999785-5-6**

Canu Publishing
(an imprint of Vocal Process Ltd)

**Vocal Process**
**For voices that *work***

# DEDICATION

I can't coach unless there's someone there.
A heartfelt thank you to all the singers, speakers, actors and teachers who have come for coaching – I literally could not have done this without you.
Thank you to my brother Mark Fisher, expert editor and fountain of knowledge on English usage (British and American).

And thank you to my wife Dr Gillyanne Kayes for the thousands of voicenerd conversations over tea in the last 20+ years, for the joy of working together in our vocal and performance technique life, and for believing in me.

# CONTENTS

# WHY DO I NEED A VOCAL COACH?

If you're a singer you enjoy singing – the feel of singing, the act of communication, and hopefully the sound you make. But there's a problem. Unlike most other musicians, you can't hear yourself properly. Because you create your voice inside your body (plus it's below and behind your ears), you can't hear the outside result that we, the listeners, can.

What you DO hear is a combination of external and internal sound. External because the sound you make bounces back to your ears from the room walls, the audience's faces, the soft furnishings, the speakers if you use them, and your ears pick up the sound waves.

Internal because the other end of your Eustachian tube (your ear canal) opens out into the back of your nose. So when you're singing, you're hearing sound waves bounce around your throat even before they come out of your mouth.

Professional voice users have an added stress – they've got to sound professionally good to their listeners – appropriate, dynamic, clear. But if you can't hear yourself (or technically, you hear yourself twice and your brain melts them together), how can you know if what you're doing is working – that you are giving your listeners the best you can give?

You need a vocal coach.

Hello, I'm Jeremy Fisher. I coach people to find their best.

Why am I qualified to do that? I'm a vocal and performance coach, a bestselling author, a creator of voice training resources, a national prizewinning professional collaborative pianist, a musical director of international tours, a singer, a voiceover artist…

I work with professional singers (classical, musical theatre, contemporary commercial, world and many other genres) and speakers (clergy, voiceover artists, actors, presenters, podcasters and webinar leaders).

This book is full of examples, case histories and stories for you to enjoy, and step-by-step techniques and tips for you to practise. They come from the knowledge and experience gained in 35+ years of professional one-to-one and group coaching, and my 16+ years of writing for blogs, national magazines and international websites.

# YES, BUT WHAT DO YOU *DO?*

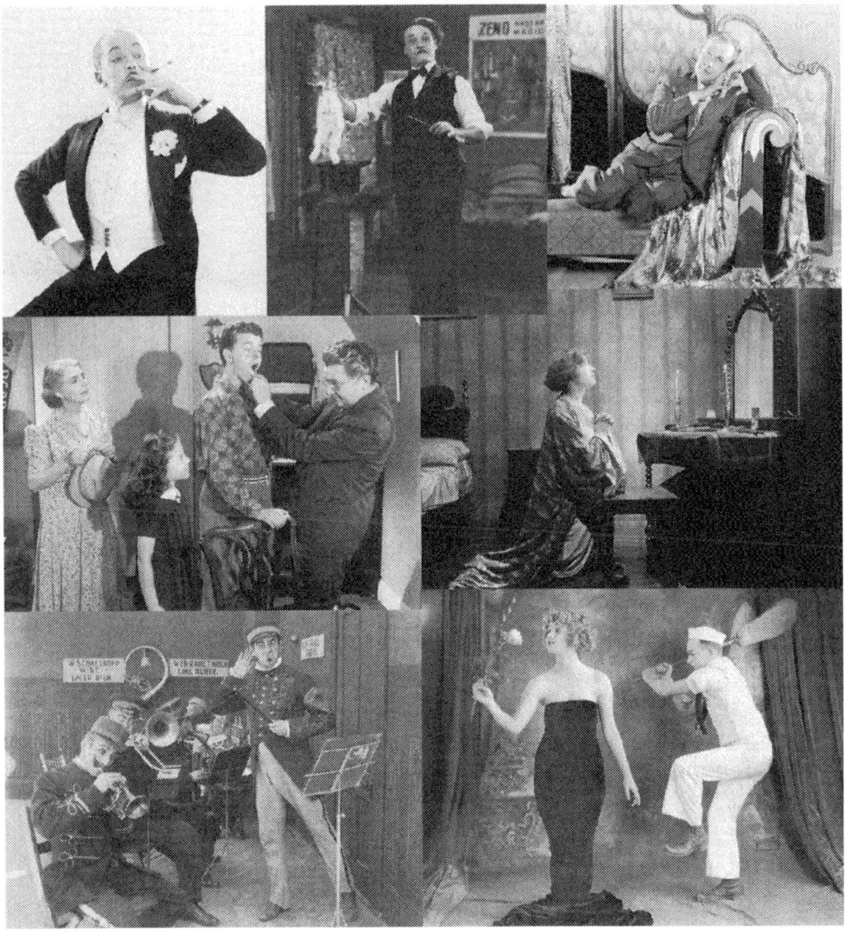


Apart from everything in the photos above? It's always been difficult to describe what I do in vocal coaching sessions (part laser-focused vocal technique, part performance goals, part energetic targeting, part magic). Let's start with some examples to whet your appetite.

The first is a little extreme, but it'll give you an idea of how I work.

## WORKING THE SONG TO SUIT THE ROLE

One of my actor/singer clients has been auditioning for the role of Mama Morton in the musical *Chicago*. She already had a song in her portfolio that she thought was suitable and came for a coaching session to polish her performance. We talked about the role of Mama Morton in general – she is the warder in a ladies' prison, and in her dialogue she alternates between support for her "family" and hard-nosed business dealing. The feel of the music is pure vaudeville, so we needed a performance that would bring all those elements together.

The song my client intended to use was a Fats Waller song, "Find out what they like" – an excellent choice. The opening lines of the chorus sum up the song: "Find out what they like and how they like it and let them have it just that way". The song is often sung as a tease, but we came up with a different subtext and scenario for the audition. We needed something very strong and direct – Mama Morton does not pull her punches and is a very powerful figure. And the result was something that is not for the easily offended!

In searching for a context for that curious combination of family and business, I came up with the madam of a brothel. This particular madam takes care of her girls but will have no nonsense – they are there to make money for her. She has seen everything, done everything, and has the t-shirt to prove it. I wanted my client to use as little movement as possible in the verse, so I asked her to perform the song as a to-camera piece. The camera is in extreme close-up, so the head fills the screen. Any extraneous movement would cause the face to disappear off camera, so the performer needs to stay very still and focused.

Moving the scenario on further, we decided that this was the filmed introduction to the brothel training video that the madam hands each new girl as they arrive. This final tweak to the scenario gave real bite to one line in the verse "Ladies! I will show you how". I predicted that my client would get the recall just on the way she said that one line. And apparently in the subsequent auditions she got to that line and the panel's heads all shot up.

Although this is an extreme example of changing the context of the song without changing the song, it was absolutely appropriate for the audition and for the role. And the client was capable of carrying the idea through. The result? She got the job.

* * *

Here are some more examples of real sessions with my singing and speaking clients.

## HE MADE IT FUN AGAIN

I worked online with another singer, Heidi Karlsson. Heidi is a very accomplished singer and often gets recalls but felt that she was getting conflicting messages in her auditions. She wanted me to pinpoint what was going wrong. I watched her sing one song and pointed out one thing (I can't reveal it in a book) that would make the difference she needed.

She said: "it was an indescribable feeling for me to have someone looking at what I do, and being able to tell me exactly what my issue is, explain it so I understand it, give exercises, try it out and BOOM, finally the problem is nailed. And I understand what to do, but most important I feel what's right and wrong now."

I normally work fast in a coaching session – and this was no exception. I had spotted the main problem within a couple of minutes and spent the rest of the hour-long session creating and applying practical exercises that defined and changed the issue.

Heidi said afterwards: "I describe it as REVOLUTIONARY. To me he nailed it completely. And he did it directly. So we had plenty of time to work on it, try different things and I ended the session with an incredible feeling of relief and happiness. He made it fun again. I always loved acting, but it turned into something anxious. Jeremy made it fun again. Magician!"

## VOICEOVER COACHING

I'm getting more speakers coming to me for vocal and performance coaching and it's fascinating to see which vocal techniques transfer to spoken voice and which don't. As we get into the higher-level business coaching, anonymity becomes more important, so I won't be naming this client.

This client in Switzerland wanted voiceover coaching. I love doing voiceovers myself so was happy to help. We worked a few sessions online and then he travelled to the UK to work with me in person in London. The scripts he was having to read were complex technical pieces with long sentences and industry jargon – they were also written by someone (not my client) using English as a second language so the scripts did not always flow. A challenge!

The particular hurdles with voiceover work include delivering sentence structure and sense without any visual cues and getting the tone right for the content. We worked on vocal technique, performance technique and tracking the sentence structure in each paragraph, extending and muting the pitch range, tempo and pauses. Here is his (typically succinct) feedback during and after the coaching sessions:

"Practical exercises to work on what I need. Always worked hard, packed every minute of every lesson. Good fun and motivating. Fantastic."

"Informative, learned a lot, worked a lot, got better. Excellent coach. Adapted lessons to a point I was struggling with. Tailor-made really. Could see results quickly. Very professional."

## VOCAL AUTHORITY AND AUTHENTICITY

The next client is a performance artist and shaman. An incredibly creative artist, we had enormous fun diagnosing and solving issues including enlarging her vocal presence, projection to a large group and adding more tonal variation to fit her storytelling.

After the first session she said: "WOW!!! I loved our Session. If you have ANY problems with your voice have a session because Jeremy can diagnose the problem, give you the solutions, and it's just such fun too! … He saw things in me that I wasn't able to see or trust. I feel really happy."

Coming from a shaman I think that is possibly the nicest feedback I've ever received.

## IS THAT WHAT HAPPENS IN YOUR VOCAL COACHING SESSIONS?

Well, each performer has their particular package of talents and energy, and every session has a different focus, depending on what each person wants to target that day. I give one-to-one lessons in person and online, on a regular basis or as a short series. I will also give single-session audition coaching for a particular job.

Swedish singer Linnéa Gustafsson booked an online coaching session for an audition. We worked the two songs she was considering for the audition, and it was clear that she was extremely experienced and a fine technical singer, but something wasn't "hitting".

During the hour session I used a combination of acting techniques, character psychology, musical structure understanding and harmonic diagnosis to help her find her story, her emotional landscape and her take" for each song.

In Linnéa's own words, it was: "A revelation. Jeremy found 'my way' of connecting with my voice and with the song, and always made sure I understood what he wanted me to do. I feel confident in the two songs I brought, but it also brought me a bigger perspective of myself as a performer."

During a coaching session we might work on a warmup appropriate to the song, technical issues with the song lyrics or the vocal tasks, performance anxiety, or clarifying the song journey. I have the most fun working with experienced singers on moulding their current repertoire to fit each audition. It's not always necessary to have a different song for every audition!

I always ask what the focus of the session is going to be. When you are working with professional actors and singers, it simply isn't appropriate to tell them what they need to learn – they are usually very focused and know exactly what they need to achieve, even if they don't know quite know how to achieve it. For audition coaching, we may tackle anything from troubleshooting specific phrases or notes, to dealing with the pianist, to how the "characters" in the song interact.

## WHO ELSE HAS COACHING SESSIONS?

In the last 12 months I've given coaching sessions online for every style of music from West End belt and current chart songs to 19th-century coloratura soprano arias and grunge, men singing women's songs, women singing men's songs and a huge number of successful auditions for current shows in the West End and on tour. I've also given career advice for conductors, MDs, singers and singing teachers using, amongst other things, live mind mapping and screen-shared apps.

My clients like the online sessions because we can time them to fit busy schedules and they don't have to leave home. I'm happy to coach singers a cappella, with backing tracks, and on a couple of memorable occasions, with live instrumentalists in the room with the singer (I coached them, too). And in 20 years of online coaching I have only had one person who didn't like the format, so we switched to in-person sessions.

* * *

In the next section you'll learn about the Singing Audition – the process you'll go through to get that coveted job in the West End, on Broadway or in a professional show. But first here's a quick breakdown of why a singer needs at least two different approaches – the technical and the inspirational – to satisfy their inner cataloguer / librarian and their inner artist.

## SINGERS NEED VOCAL TECHNIQUE AND PERFORMANCE SKILLS

My wife Dr Gillyanne Kayes and I were talking about how singers learn. We've seen the difference between a singer or actor following a technical instruction, and actually knowing how to apply it to improve singing.

This struck a chord with me because one of my favourite instructions having taught a technique is "that's good, now make it *work*". Meaning, even if you can do the technique or make the sound, you need to make it your own.

It seems that there are at least two aspects to a singer – the singer's "intellect" and the singer's "performer", or the separation of vocal technique and performance skills.

### *Working With the Singer's "Intellect"*

When we teach a technique, we're working with the singer's intellect. The intellect builds a catalogue of possible personal vocal options to be used. The catalogue can be added to, altered and expanded with new sounds, vocal techniques and concepts. In a singing lesson you're adding a new item to your vocal catalogue, and you do it using both repetition and understanding. This is what a singing lesson is really about, the technique of creating sounds.

It's essential to feed your catalogue with new sounds and techniques to keep yourself current. But that isn't using your creative being.

### *Working With the Singer's "Performer"*

This is where the performer then takes over. The performer takes the thoughts, the character, the music, the lyrics and the rhythm that are in the catalogue and makes them come alive. The performer in us will use *anything* in the catalogue to embody and express its ideas. Whenever you add something new to the catalogue, the performer can grab that and use it, often without you thinking about it – this is not intellectual but instinctive.

And I believe the two are distinguishable. we all know of "talented" people who have not yet matured in their performing. Usually there is something "magic" that is recognizable – it could be that the performer part is ready to fly, but the technical catalogue is not yet broad enough to encompass everything the performer wishes to do. Likewise we can recognize the technically accomplished singer who just doesn't touch us in any way emotionally. The catalogue is well-honed, but the performer does not fly.

I have a background as an accompanist, collaborative pianist and musical director. I'm used to assessing the whole performance, finding what the "performer" wants to do and helping it happen. The real skill of the coach is to recognize what already works for the performer, and which areas can be stimulated to work better *for that particular performer.*

In effect, this is what a coaching session is about, encouraging the performer to experiment with different uses of their inbuilt catalogue.

This whole conversation came about because of one of our clients: she is very capable of adding to her catalogue of sounds and will copy, repeat and understand.

The interesting part is when she starts to perform – we see her going into a completely different part of her brain. And it's so far away from her "intellect" part that the two don't really connect. The technique that she has just mastered intellectually doesn't appear in her performing.

We've been working on connecting her "intellect" with her "performer" and it's really beginning to pay dividends. That's really where the consistent performance magic lies.

But that's a whole other story!

# THE SINGING AUDITION – SOME ADVICE

In this chapter, I break down the process of auditioning for a musical or professional show. All the major shows in London's West End use a version of this process, so read on to find out what happens and how to work each audition stage to your advantage…

## AUDITIONING FOR MUSICALS: THE CATTLE CALL

Here's the first of three articles I wrote on the process of auditioning for a West End or Broadway show. If you want to audition for musicals on Broadway or in the West End, and you don't have an agent, you need to go to the open call, known as the Cattle Call. This article describes the cattle call, what you need to take and what you need to do to succeed.

There are new musicals being written every year, and long-running shows being recast regularly. But there are thousands of actor-singer-dancers seeking work in musical theatre. You want to be heard for roles in these shows, but you don't have an agent. Where do you start? Every year, production companies run open calls. They are particularly useful if the show is new or in an unusual genre (grunge / folk / rock or Tuvan throat singing), if there is a serious lack of actors with the relevant casting requirements (ethnic casting or tightrope juggling), or if the casting directors simply want to know what's out there at the moment. Open calls are usually advertised in the theatre press (*The Stage* newspaper in the UK is an example). The open call can be quite a demoralizing process (not for nothing are they called "cattle calls"), so this article will help you prepare for them.

The first thing you'll see when you arrive is a long queue. Depending on how popular the show is, the queue could be three times round the block, or just a small crowd. Be prepared to stand in the queue for several hours. Even 15 years ago, professional singer friends of mine were kept waiting for 7 hours on the auditions for nuns in *The Sound of Music*. What should you carry with you? Your resume or CV and a photograph are essential. If the photograph is not attached, make sure that both the resume and photograph have your name and contact details on. Photographs and CV details often get separated, and it would be horrible if the panel remembered your face but then couldn't find your contact details on the photo. A bottle of water is vital, and either a book or an mp3 player is useful to while away the hours.

You will give your name to the auditions usher or stage door manager, and the audition begins. If you're lucky, you'll have about 2 minutes to get on stage, introduce yourself and do your audition. If you're unlucky, you'll have 16 bars. If you're unlucky, they will ask you for your best single phrase. How do you deal with this? Remember that the purpose of this audition is NOT to get the job! If you're up against 1,000 people or more, nothing you can do will make you stand out enough to be offered the job on the spot. Your mission is to get asked back to the first call (the first invited call, as opposed to the cattle call). Therefore, your task is to appear professional, calm and focused. That's it.

If you look professional (dress appropriately, perform to a good standard, interact well with the panel) you will be noticed. If you seem calm you will score points too – cattle calls are difficult situations with a lot of "unknowns" – such as not knowing what time you're going to perform – and a vast number of people breathing down your neck! If you are focused, you'll be able to sing your piece to the best of your ability, and lock into the character immediately. Being focused really "reads" well on a theatre stage, so the panel will notice very quickly how well you do.

When I'm coaching for the 16-bar audition, the key is to practise EVERYTHING. The walk in, the hello, the piece announcement, giving the pianist the music (or the backing track), the getting into focus, the 16 bars (decided beforehand, please!), and the exit. Everything matters, including the way you talk to the auditions usher. I work to help you choose song extracts that show your best (and it's not necessarily your loudest or highest), and to sing those extracts to the best of your ability. Notice I haven't said what you should sing!

Ultimately, in a cattle call your choice of song is less important than how you sing it. I have been on cattle calls where actors singing the weirdest songs have been called back for the next audition, simply because they sang it very well. In a situation like this you want to stack the dice in your favour as much as possible. Take a piece you know well – that way if nerves strike, you will still feel secure in your song.

Panels find cattle calls just as horrible as you do, and believe me, they breathe a sigh of relief when someone professional, calm and focused turns up. There usually are three piles in front of a cattle call casting panel. Yes, No, Maybe. The only pile you want to be in is the Yes pile. And if you give a clear, focused, professional performance and follow the rules in this article, you're much more likely to get to sing in the next round and stay in the Yes pile.

## AUDITIONING FOR MUSICALS: WHAT TO DO IN THE FIRST AUDITION

Here's the second of three articles I wrote on the process of auditioning for a West End or Broadway show. For actors, singers and dancers, auditioning for musicals is a way of life. But what if this is your first musicals audition? How do you behave, what do you have to do, and how should you prepare? This article focuses on the first (private) audition in the process of auditioning for a musical.

You've got an audition for a musical theatre show. What do you do and what do you aim to achieve? First, let's explore what an audition is for. For the casting panel, it's an opportunity to see new people, or to remind themselves of familiar people. It's a chance to see who and what is out there, to make decisions about casting, and to match up different actors to make a company. For you, it's an opportunity to let the casting panel get to know your performing ability, hear you sing and see you in your choice of character.

Now let's explore what the first audition is not. It's not a true performance – the audience doesn't applaud, they haven't paid to see you, there are no lights, no costumes and no makeup (other than what you have brought with you). It's not a complete show either, as the panel will expect to watch you come in as yourself, then change into character in front of them.

And finally, the first audition will not get you the job. That may sound odd, but in reality, West End auditions and Broadway auditions can go on for up to nine recalls spread over several months. And on large-scale musicals you won't be cast on the strength of your first audition. Remember that the company wants to know how skilled you are, how well you inhabit the character, how well you deal with being on stage, and whether you are the appropriate professional level for the production. The key points are to appear professional, well-prepared and confident with your material. And for the first audition it's vital for an actor, singer or dancer to use song material that's suitable for their casting, voice and abilities.

Let's examine some of the common mistakes that auditionees make.

Singers might be confident of how they sound, but don't think about character or story. In musical theatre, this is a complete no-no. Yes, you might have a lovely voice, but we're interested in your character's journey through the song. Musical theatre differs from opera or song recital in that the music serves and heightens the text, and characterization is vital.

Conversely, actors might be very confident of their subtext and characterization but might not have a solid vocal technique. While strong character decisions can carry an actor through dodgy vocalizing, remember that this is a musical genre, and usually you will be performing eight shows a week or more. For your own sanity (and the sanity of those around you), it's imperative that your vocal technique is strong and clear enough for you to sustain and repeat what you are doing accurately and without strain. If not, a single cold can knock your performance sideways.

For dancers who are used to expressing themselves in movement, using words and music can be a real challenge. And since many dancers start very young, learning a solid technique in a new discipline can seem like a mountainous task. It's important for dancers to find teachers of voice, text, or singing who can adapt their teaching styles to the dance-trained body and mind. Choose repertoire that you have a physical connection with, pieces that you feel they can play with. And don't be afraid to move during an audition – you don't have to stay rooted to the spot!

When coaching a singer-actor-dancer for the first call, my sessions usually focus on choosing repertoire that suits your physical and energetic casting, and helping you find (and maintain) your very best performance of it. We also deal with the various problems surrounding auditions using your own-choice songs: presenting YOUR version of the song to the pianist in 15 seconds or less, how to find the focus of your song and get into character instantly, interacting with the panel, even altering your performance of your familiar repertoire to suit the style of that particular show.

Sometimes you can alter the subtext or storyline of a song to fit the show that is currently casting. If you must sing just a 16-bar excerpt or a cut version, your storyline will be different anyway – it's not a good idea to try playing the full song journey if you're only singing half the song! You might focus on the one aspect of the character that appears in that extract, or impose a journey on the music, or bring an event that happens later in the full song into that particular musical moment. If you are using the same song for the cattle call and the first full audition (also known as the privates), you will almost certainly need more than one mental map of the song.

Once you have found good songs, a session from a qualified coach can help you find your own version of the material, and lead you to create living, sustainable characterizations that use your best talents and assets. With songs that match your casting, good performance skills and a professional attitude, you will definitely be noticed. And what do you aim to achieve in the first audition?

To get the first recall.

## AUDITIONING FOR MUSICALS: WORKING THROUGH THE RECALL SYSTEM

Here's the third of three articles I wrote on the process of auditioning for a West End or Broadway show. As a vocal coach specializing in successful singing auditions, I know that the auditioning process can be either a dismal failure that actors want to hide from, or an opportunity to present your work to the same knowledgeable people in a well-defined sequence of events. This article describes working through the recall system, and how a coach can help performers through the different recall stages.

When an actor, singer or dancer auditions for a show, it is very rare that they are cast on the first hearing. With thousands of actors, singers and dancers looking for work, the recall system is a necessary evil. (One of our clients in the UK had to go through nine recalls – all at her own expense – before being cast in the show.) This article describes the different stages of auditioning, and how I coach performers through the system.

I'm assuming that you have either succeeded in or bypassed the preliminary stage of auditioning, the open call (or cattle call), and completed the first full call. Getting a recall means that the company has decided you might fit the part and are at approximately the right level for them. They want to find out more about you and how you deal with the material in the show. They will usually give you music and script for the roles they want you to audition for. If the production company haven't given any music or instructions, but has asked you to sing your own choice for them again, my advice is NOT to take new songs "to show something different" but to polish the same songs that were sung in the first audition. I also advise wearing the same clothes – after all, it's that song, that performance and that clothing that was appropriate enough to get you the recall, so why jeopardize your chances?

During a coaching session for auditions, we focus on the song, the character and the story – what's the package that we're selling? This technique, used for first auditions with your own choice of song, can be applied to the recall. We'll explore the songs the casting panel has provided, identify the style elements of the show and incorporate them into the song (and your voice). We'll also nail the personality aspects of the character, and experiment with dialogue and scenes to carry the character through singing AND speaking to produce a cohesive performance.

That's the first major hurdle. But the second recall is different again. By this time, you will probably have been given not just the music but also some clues or advice on how the company wants the character to be played. In coaching for the second recall, we might experiment with different readings of the song based on different subtexts. It's important in the second recall that you give a clear performance but can remain flexible as an actor.

The third recall is usually a more flexible event. You now know that you are at the right level and appropriate for the role. Often in the third recall the director and musical director will work with you in detail. This is the time to listen and experiment! Occasionally other auditioning actors will be brought in to "match up" a potential cast. My coaching sessions for the third recall are much more focused, using information and hints given by the panel.

For example, working on auditions for the musical *Spring Awakening* recently, one of my clients was looking at three different roles and had been given very specific instructions from the directors for all three songs. We worked on more aggression and bite in the consonants for one character, a more fluid, lyrical feel with some musical style tweaks for the second, and a hypnotic, sexually dominant feel for the third.

Another client was working on recalls for *Mamma Mia!* and was up for two of the three leading ladies. We worked on the dialogue for each character, identifying and shaping the differences between the two roles, finding the essence of their speech patterns, speed of delivery, pitch range and characterization. Then we carried those differences into the songs to give a complete, identifiable package for each of the leads.

By the time you get to the fourth, fifth or sixth recall, you will have a relationship with the casting panel, and they have more time to discuss what they want to experience from you. You should be able to find out if there are any weaknesses in your presentation, and what you can do about it. Experimentation is vital here so know your material!

Occasionally at this point, it's less about you and more about the casting panel disagreeing about what the role requires. Perhaps a show originates on Broadway and comes over to the West End (or vice versa). In these cases, there is often an American casting contingent who might have very different ideas. Just stay calm and do what you do. Be prepared to change everything that you have done so far. Stay focused and open, and listen very carefully to what you are being told. In the rare event that you receive conflicting information, follow the advice of the person with the highest authority! And if you don't get any further in this particular journey, remember that the casting panel in your country has already approved your performing and will remember you for other shows.

Auditioning for jobs is a fact of life for the actor-singer-dancer. Once you become more successful at singing auditions, casting directors start to see you in other roles and you can bypass the first stages of auditioning (although even for the stars auditioning never goes away – "Would you like to pop in for a chat and a little sing?"). Landing a role in a Broadway show or getting a West End lead can be incredibly rewarding. Working the Recall System in this way can help you understand the process and get you there quicker.

* * *

In the next chapter we're going to eavesdrop inside my studio on actual coaching sessions. I'm sharing what each singer wanted to achieve, how I identify the actual problems (not the symptoms), and the techniques used to get that singer back on track.

# THE SINGING AUDITION – EAVESDROPPING ON COACHING SESSIONS

Someone once said "you make these things up". Well no, everything described in these chapters has happened, every coaching session describes real people with real problems, from *Frozen* in late 2019 all the way back to *Lord of The Rings* in the 2007 West End production and beyond. I often write up sessions the same day if there's something that happens that I think other singers would find interesting or useful. The 3.5-hour train journey home from London to the Welsh borders is the perfect time to put thoughts down on paper. So here are a handful of my sessions. I've mixed audition advice, performing tips, vocal technique and exercise descriptions with stories from my studio.

## HOW DO YOU FIND A 16-BAR SINGING AUDITION PERFORMABLE UNIT?

The 16-bar audition is a newish feature of life as an actor-singer-dancer in the West End. It's a way for the casting panel to see new people but without taking the time to hear whole songs. The point for the actor is to show a very brief snapshot of their character choices and story and to get the call-back.

When I help people choose songs for specific auditions, I look for several different ways to match the prospective musical. It could be something by the same composer or the same era (music style). It could be something with the same emotional arc for the character (storyline) or the same type of drama/comedy (energy and "flavour"). It could even be something written in a very different style but that we can change to fit the character "type".

One of my most successful morphs was getting one of my experienced clients to audition with a music-hall song. It was a romantic song written for a young ingenue, but I advised her to sing it in the style of Madame Thénadier. It was shocking, hilarious and got her the recall and the job.

### *A Real-Life Example*

In one of my coaching sessions in London, a client needs an audition song for *Frozen*. He's aiming at the role of Olaf and we need a song that would work, that's close enough to the character, but that isn't from *Frozen*.

My client has the idea of using one of Donkey's songs from *Shrek* – a great choice for situation and lyrics but it's far too long and the character doesn't quite match. He needs a 16-bar cut version that would stand up by itself. He also needs to show the casting panel *enough* hints of the character of Olaf that they could see him playing the role, without singing songs from the show.

### *16 Bars?*

Let's digress for a moment and ask the questions "What does a 16-bar version need", and "Does it really need to be 16 bars?"

The 16 bars of a ballad last a lot longer than the 16 bars of a patter song. When Gillyanne and I do our Successful Singing Auditions masterclasses, we tend to refer to the 16-bar cut as a singing audition performable unit. This takes away the desire to count bars and stop the music at unfortunate or bizarre points (and yes, I've witnessed a lot of those in auditions).

It also deals with the question of whether the 16 bars includes piano parts or not – a singing audition performable unit is complete in itself and works successfully without the rest of the song so you can include as much of the piano part as you need to start and finish the unit tastefully.

### *The Singing Audition Performable Unit*

What makes a singing audition performable unit? It depends very much on the style of the song, what you want to feature and the requirements of the role you're auditioning for. I rarely start an audition performance unit at the beginning of the song, and I don't always include the loudest bits either. Usually, I will choose a part of the song that reflects the character we're aiming at. For my *Frozen* client, we decide that we really did need a "beginning, middle and end". That meant the opening of the song, a recognizable part of the verse/chorus and a finish.

My task is to find a *drastic* cut that works well and to help him move his characterization from Donkey towards Olaf. We start with a sing-through of the whole song to gauge what works well already and if there are any sections that we could immediately cut or ignore. Then we start looking for some fairly drastic cuts.

I suggest we start at the beginning with the colla voce (follow the singer) section, sing the first 8 bars of the verse and jump slam-bang into the big finish, cutting about eight pages and four key changes. The way we work it, I don't even need to rewrite any of the piano part! We have exactly what's required to show character, storyline and vocal capability.

Now to count the bars. Ah… 27 bars in total. But the unit is so good and so complete that I think it's worth checking the timing. Sometimes if you have a lot more than 16 bars it helps to know how long you're singing (so you can tell the panel if they ask). We think a total of 1 minute and 6 seconds was fine for a 16-bar audition, so we go ahead with this cut version.

### *Morphing the Song – the Skilled Bit*

Now we need to change the character to fit the audition. We start with choosing keywords for the existing version of the song and character. Donkey is spiky, somewhat sarcastic with a healthy dose of James Brown. Focusing on the new character, the keywords we decide on for Olaf are gentle, naïve, excitable and slightly confused. We take all the hard-edged sounds out and add a gentle excitability, together with more fear/desperation that he might be left behind. It means we can introduce a different type of comedy into the performance that works well for the character without losing the drive of the song.

That whole process takes less than half an hour, so we have time to work two more songs for other auditions.

Client, sorted.

PS Morphing a song that you already know towards your next audition – that's one of my favourite things to do. If you have auditions coming up and you want to get the recall, book a session with me online or in London.

www.DrGillyanneKayesJeremyFisherInspirationSession.as.me

* * *

## HOW DANCE LANGUAGE CAN CHANGE YOUR SINGING

I work with many dancers who sing and singers who dance. The triple threat in musical theatre (actor, singer, dancer) is fast becoming the norm.

My client this morning is a triple threat who thinks in dance terms. She's a dancer through and through. So how could I as a vocal coach tap into a dancer's wide and deep knowledge of their craft?

In today's lesson I set my client a challenge: to sing the first 16 bars of four songs, one after another, and to "hit the ground running". Her task was to find the storyline, emotion and mood of each character in the first bar.

Things were going quite well, and she was producing good performances, but I felt I could get something stronger from her.

### *The Audition Technique*

In my Answers On A Postcard technique, the singer chooses a phrase that she can use mentally at the beginning of the song to get her straight into character. (See Webinar 5 "Exams, Auditions and Competitions" for how this works). My client had just been telling me about a TV series she was in charting the history of dance, so I decided to extend the technique. I suggested she think of the characteristics of different dance styles to incorporate them into her performance.

The song was "Stop and See Me" from *Weird Romance*, and the style I suggested to bring to the song mentally was hip-hop. She didn't move a muscle or change her position in any way, but the difference in the characterization was extraordinary. She became stronger, cockier, yet much more vulnerable. Perfect for the song. The reading got deeper, more truthful and infinitely more moving. I felt I was witnessing an aspect of her really for the first time. It went beyond "finding my version of this song" and became "finding *myself* in the song". When I saw that she had completely understood the concept, we moved on to the concept of using costume as a creative kicker.

"Gorgeous" from *The Apple Tree* is a "Cinderella" song about a young woman who sees herself in beautiful clothes for the first time. We started with imagining her in the My Fair Lady Ascot costume, but the song also needs a more earthy sense of humour. So, we kept the scenario and added Miranda Hart in a wedding dress (if you haven't seen the Miranda BBC comedy series, check it out).

"Someday" from *The Wedding Singer* became a number from Grease with bobby sox, a dirndl skirt and a vision of Teen Angel.

"God Help The Outcasts" became an Eco-warrior with dreads, occupying the cathedral steps (this actually happened at St Paul's Cathedral recently, although I'm not sure they sang numbers from *Notre Dame…*)

The term **"performance magic"** is horribly overused, but when you see someone transform for the first time into a totally different character, in songs they've known and sung for years, there's no other phrase that fits.

Job done.

*   *   *

## HELP! MY ACCOMPANIST ISN'T LISTENING!

It happened to me in my first college audition as an oboist.

You may not know that, back in the 19th century, I played the oboe, and applied to the Conservatoires in London, Birmingham and Manchester as a first-study oboist. This was my first audition in Manchester. I had gone through the speeds with the accompanist (andante and allegro for the Bellini oboe concerto). The first movement is long, long phrases, and the second is a chirpy staccato frivol.

In the audition I nearly died. And I think I mean that literally. The opening movement was soooooo slooowwwwww I was on the floor. And I was determined to play all the phrases in one breath. I know more now. The second movement was so fast that my fingers and tongue were a blur. At just 17 I didn't know how to deal with that, but it must be said that I rise to a challenge, and I managed to get in all the notes, all the articulation, and all the breaths. I was offered one of only three places at the college.

### *Dealing With an Awkward Pianist*

Now if that situation arises for my clients, I take time to help them deal with it. It came up today with one of my clients. She has been working away from London for several weeks and came for a "wash and brush-up" vocal and performance session. The first 10 minutes of the session was spent talking through some of the auditions she's done between the end of the last job and that day. Although talking in a lesson might feel like a waste of time (and money), it was vital that I heard what had been happening for her out in the real world.

In fact, I learned a very interesting piece of information about one of her songs. She does "I'm a Woman (W.O.M.A.N)" as one of her character up-tempo songs and had had a problem at the last audition. The pianist had not played the accompaniment in rhythm, and it had completely thrown her. The thing about this piano part is that there are very few notes at all in it. Most of it is silence. All it really consists of is rock "stabs" at the end of every 2 bars. The singer has a fast string of words (not necessarily even sung) between the stabs. Now the whole thing is in tempo, but if as a pianist you are used to playing Handel recitatives, you'll see the written rests and ignore them. Because in Handel recitative the rests are not there to be counted or played, they are there to make up the proper time of the bar between notes and can safely be ignored.

Before all the opera singers start writing to me – again – yes, I know that *accompanied* recitative with orchestra **is** played in tempo. But in rock music or Motown, that simply isn't the case. It's as if there's a drumbeat going throughout. So, the "down and dirty" pulse is there all the time. Think of the Diet Coke television ad with the song "I Just Want to Make Love to You" and you will know what I mean.

### *Duetting With a Stranger*

So back to the client. What I discovered is that she didn't know what to do if the pianist got her music wrong in an audition. This is a situation that happens a lot. After all, as an actor or singer you are "duetting with a stranger" whenever you do a singing audition. There's a whole section on duetting with a stranger in the *Successful Singing Auditions* book. So being the good, supportive teacher that I am, I made her go through the piece again, and I played as badly as I could.

We decided that the problem was that the pianist did not know the piece or the style, and just needed guidance. In this piece the "down and dirty rhythm" is so strong that there is an easy solution. Click your fingers to the beat. If you hear the pianist doing something strange with the rhythm while you are singing, just start clicking and swinging and he should pick it up. Be sure to make it part of your character's persona; don't just glare at him and stamp your foot in time.

We experimented with me playing faster, slower or arrhythmically so that she could experience how each one felt, and how easy or difficult it was to take control and alter what was happening. As it happens, she was so secure on the speed and feel of the piece that it was very easy to follow her clicking and swinging, and all was well.

I also suggested that in her 15 seconds of talking to the pianist beforehand (speed, feel, map-reading advice) she added "This piece is absolutely in tempo". We thought that would probably do the trick.

Incidentally, she got the job. Sometimes you just can't tell how it's gone.

One word of caution: if you do come across pianists who puts their head down and close their ears, and nothing has changed within about 5 seconds of you starting to click, there's only one thing you can do… Abandon hope. A three-ton truck in the small of the back wouldn't shift them Just grit your teeth and do your own thing.

At least everyone else will have them too.

* * *

## FITTING THE SONG TO THE SINGER

I spend a good deal of my time as a musical theatre vocal coach helping my clients adapt the song to the audition.

After we had sorted out dealing with the pianist (see previous section, "Help! My accompanist isn't listening!"), I decided to work on matching the song to the client and her casting.

This client has quite a wide range of casting possibilities. It's impossible to find one song that will fit all those characters, but this song can work in more than one way.

The Cockney, the American and the Jamaican...

Bearing in mind that the rhythm and speed of the song are pretty much set in advance, we changed the character who was singing it. The first version was the one she had used in the previous audition – the Cockney. The director had given her a clue as to where he wanted to go with the casting, so my client picked up the information and ran with it.

Changing the accent to proper Cockney (East London, born within the sound of Bow Bells) made her characterization sharper, slightly more up-front and sassier. With this client it also had the effect of changing the body posture and body language, and the sound she made. It doesn't always work that well! For the technically minded among you, she used a thicker fold mass for a stronger, slightly darker version of her standard chest voice, slightly more edgy brightness, less breath flow and more pitch drop offsets with shorter notes. The second version was American businesswoman. More brightness, slightly thinner folds, more clipped delivery, and a completely different body language – tighter, more upright and a higher energy.

The third version (my personal favourite) was the Jamaican nurse. The Jamaican accent caused the words to have a different accentuation – almost as many glottals as the Cockney, ironically. The body language became heavier and more into the ground and the sound got slightly thicker and more relaxed with a wider vocal tract, with more underlying humour.

I chose these three types because I've heard her audition speeches and I wanted to match her sung performances with spoken ones. I believe it's important in an audition to give a matching package. Beware of the "I can do this, I can do that" auditionee – showing everything can end up causing confusion.

Because we've done this type of work before in lessons, when the director gave her completely different acting cues to work with, she was able to change in an instant the vocal characterization she had prepared without either throwing her concentration or upsetting the feel of the song itself. I'm doing a lot of this type of work with my clients now, and the recall rate in auditions has certainly increased.

* * *

## "I NEED A SONG THAT SHOWS EVERYTHING"

One of my clients arrived with the intention of auditioning for four different musicals in one audition.

The panel she was playing to was ostensibly there to cast *Avenue Q*, but many of the panellists have interests in other shows. She had decided to aim for the four main shows that they work on – *Avenue Q*, *Mary Poppins*, *Phantom of the Opera* and *Les Misérables*. Now in terms of style, these four are about as far apart as you can get and still be called musicals. OK, granted there are no rock-based shows there, but it's still quite a mixed bag of music styles. *Phantom* is operetta / contemporary lyrical, *Les Misérables* is what we call in the *Successful Singing Auditions* book a Verismo musical (gritty and dramatic), *Mary Poppins* is an old-fashioned classic book musical (think Richard Rodgers music, although updated by Styles and Drew), and *Avenue Q* is a popular, Disney-type musical with a cabaret feel and satirical lyrics.

In other words, there are no two songs in existence that will cover all those bases. This is a problem I often see in my studio. "I need a song that shows everything". Well first, there isn't one, and second, if you try to show everything in 3 minutes, you'll end up showing nothing particularly well.

In this case, we decided that the client wanted to aim for the more classic end of the spectrum, so we chose songs to target *Mary Poppins* and *Phantom of the Opera.*

### *Auditioning for* Phantom Of The Opera

*Phantom* is an interesting one. Having been part of many thousands of auditions for *Phantom* in London, I know that there is quite a wide range of repertoire that can be used. Successful singers in the past have used opera, operetta and Gilbert and Sullivan, or popular ballads, or standards with a story such as Gershwin or Cole Porter. With the client aiming at Christine, we decided on "How Could I Ever Know", from *The Secret Garden.* This is a lyrical ballad with a reasonably wide range. The role of Christine was written specifically for Sarah Brightman's voice, and although Christine famously has a high E to sing and a cadenza going to a D6, most of the role sits in the middle and lower part of the range. There is quite a lot of narrative writing, and the song from *The Secret Garden* covers this.

You can often match songs from different musicals (or even decades) by choosing something to focus on. In this case, I chose Christine's dressing-room scene as a basis for repertoire choice. She sings to Raoul about "Little Lottie", a storybook tale that reflects her own life, and tells him of her new teacher. The text style (both narrative and personal), vocal range and the general feel of the writing has similarities to the song "How Could I Ever Know". I will also consider not just the vocal range but the tessitura. This is the area within the vocal range in which most of the song sits. If the total range was, say, low C to upper G but most of the song sits between low D and the D above (with only a few upper and lower notes), the tessitura is said to be D-D. Again, the tessiturae of both songs are similar, so this together with the feel and emotion of the writing, makes one a good choice for the other's audition.

### *Auditioning for* Mary Poppins

With the ballad chosen for the *Phantom of the Opera* audition (see previous section), we turned our attention to the *Mary Poppins* song. We were looking for an up-tempo song with a classic-book feel. As well as the usual show songs, Gershwin, Porter and Novello are usually a useful source of classic material.

The client already had a song in her database that we both felt would fit the bill. "Don't Look At Me That Way" is a song by Cole Porter from the show *Paris*. It's an up-tempo, flirtatious song saying, "I love whatever you do, and I particularly lose control when you look at me like that." This client is Canadian and is quite used to singing with an American accent. However, for *Mary Poppins* I felt it best to sing with an English accent. We spent a couple of sessions exploring the differences between the accents. She is remarkably quick, and after two sessions had the accent just about nailed. The dialect for this show is an interesting one – it's not hyperlect, and it's not quite Standard British (as I hear it), but a gentle cross between the two.

Having nailed the accent, we focused on the character. *Mary Poppins* is not flirtatious, although she can be "fun". So I made one small adjustment to the song: The opening lines of the chorus (I think you're great, I think you're grand, And I don't mind if you hold my hand) were sung straight, but the change came in the title line (But don't look at me that way). Instead of being sung as a come-on, we changed the subtext to "Bert, stop that at once!" it gave much more of the flavour of the British nanny (think Jo Frost in the television series Supernanny) and worked very well in the song.

This is the kind of work I really enjoy – altering the song subtext to suit the job you are auditioning for. I'll be returning to more coaching session descriptions like this later in the book.

* * *

# COFFEE BREAK

Time for a coffee break and a quiz. "World Voice Day" is April 16th and we usually create something special for it. This fun quiz comes from way back in 2014 and is all about your voice. When we launched it, we had over 450 actors, singers, dancers, teachers and therapists complete it straight away. But you'd be surprised how many people got some of the answers wrong.

# OUR "WORLD VOICE DAY" QUIZ

1. **A voice needs: vocal folds, a resonating space and…**
    a. Chocolate
    b. A glass of port
    c. Breath
2. **Where is your larynx?**
    a. In my throat
    b. In my boots
    c. We don't talk about that in polite society
3. **In order to sing higher you have to…**
    a. Inhale helium
    b. Vibrate your vocal folds faster
    c. Engage your gluteus maximus
4. **The sound comes out…**
    a. Of my mouth or nose (or both)
    b. Only after 11am
    c. Of the top of my head
5. **Your diaphragm…**
    a. Can be felt by putting your hand on your abdomen
    b. Can be felt by putting your hands around your waist
    c. Can't be felt from the outside
6. **The diaphragm is used for…**
    a. Breathing in
    b. Carrying the shopping
    c. Birth control
7. **The only thing in your vocal tract that doesn't move is…**
    a. Your hard palate
    b. Your larynx
    c. Your eyebrows
8. **In order to stop nasality you need to…**
    a. Close the doorway into the nose
    b. Make a bigger space in the mouth
    c. Pray
9. **Men's vocal folds are…**
    a. Usually longer and thicker than women's
    b. Prone to saying things they don't mean
    c. A complete mystery

**10. Your voice will be healthier if every day you drink…**
   a. A litre of strong black coffee
   b. A bottle of claret
   c. About 2 litres of plain water

**11. Most songs cover**
   a. 1.5 octaves, that's comfortable for me
   b. 5 notes, small but perfectly formed
   c. 5 octaves, I put all my whistle and creak notes into every song

**12. A professional voice user…**
   a. Has studied voice for years
   b. Uses their voice for work more than 5 hours a day
   c. Competes on X-Factor

**13. Having a healthy voice means…**
   a. You can sing higher and louder than anyone else in your country
   b. You can express yourself clearly without getting a tired voice
   c. You have your own YouTube channel

[Answers on next page.]

## ANSWERS TO THE "WORLD VOICE DAY" QUIZ

1. **A voice needs: vocal folds, a resonating space and…**
   **c. Breath to get the vocal folds vibrating.**
2. **Where is your larynx?**
   **a. In my throat.**
   Although we still hear about singing teachers who refuse to talk about the larynx saying it plays no part in singing…
3. **In order to sing higher you have to…**
   **b. Vibrate your vocal folds faster.**
   It's the speed of the vocal folds that dictate what pitch you sing. Engaging your gluteus maximus (the buttocks) is not essential for singing (and certainly not good for singing and walking at the same time…)
   And if you want to inhale helium, check out this wonderful YouTube clip from King's College Choir
   https://www.youtube.com/watch?v=ukDAfF0-8q8
4. **The sound comes out…**
   **a. Of my mouth or nose (or both).**
   Mouth for a clear vowel, nose for an /ng/ and both for a nasal vowel (think the French word "bien").
   Sorry people, but they're the only exit holes in the vocal tract. And for the six people who said, "of the top of my head", it's unlikely unless trepanning is back in fashion.
5. **Your diaphragm…**
   **c. Can't be felt from the outside.**
   A startling 129 people got this wrong, and we know this is a common misunderstanding, so I'll explain.
   The diaphragm sits high up inside the ribcage. At the front it connects to the bottom of the breastbone (at the xiphoid process) and follows the shape of the ribs down and around. But since it's a double-dome shape it lives up inside the ribcage, almost at nipple level and never reaches abdominal or waist level.
   When the diaphragm contracts downwards to pull air into the lungs, there's no real room for it to move. So the abdominal contents have to be displaced downwards. What you're feeling when you put your hand on your abdomen or

waist is not your diaphragm but your abdominal wall muscles releasing and the abdominal contents moving down and forwards out of the way. The diaphragm just doesn't come out of its rib-shell.

6. **The diaphragm is used for…**
   **a. Breathing in.**
   Surprisingly, not everyone got this right. The diaphragm is a muscle of inspiration (you use it to breathe in). You don't really use it to breathe out, or carry the shopping, and the diaphragm for birth control is a whole different ballgame…
7. **The only thing in your vocal tract that doesn't move is…**
   **a. Your hard palate.**
   It's the only bone structure in this list and forms part of your skull.
   Only 19 people thought your larynx doesn't move. But it needs to move up and down hundreds of times a day to swallow – that's why it's slung from muscles and ligaments rather than attached directly to another bone. And if you decide to fix your larynx in one position to sing (and we don't recommend it), it's a personal choice rather than a physical necessity.
   And 37 people said your eyebrows, but of course your eyebrows aren't in your vocal tract and have nothing to do with the sound you make (unless you use wiggling your eyebrows as a method of creating vibrato…)
8. **In order to stop nasality you need to…**
   **a. Close the doorway into the nose.**
   You have two entrances/exits in the vocal tract, your mouth and your nose. The soft palate acts as a doorway between the two spaces – it opens to allow air in and out through the nose and closes to block the nasal spaces off. You do this when you swallow anything, otherwise it would all come down your nose instead of going into the oesophagus.
   A total of 80 people thought that making a bigger space in the mouth would stop nasality. Ironically, given that muscles for the soft palate (palatoglossus) connect to the tongue, you're MORE likely to become nasal if you make a bigger space inside, as that usually involves pulling the tongue

down/back, potentially pulling the soft palate down with it. There is some confusion about the causes and fixes for nasality in the singing and speaking world, which is why we created an entire technique video for nasality and the soft palate!

9. **Men's vocal folds are…**
   **b. Prone to saying things they don't mean**
   Just kidding, it's
   **a. – usually longer and thicker than women's**
10. **Your voice will be healthier if every day you drink…**
    **c. About 2 litres of plain water.**
    The advice varies on the amount (The British Voice Association leaflet recommends 6–8 glasses a day), but water will hydrate your body tissues, and this contributes to healthy voice. Incidentally, the water doesn't touch your vocal folds directly – if it did, you'd probably choke. Apologies to the slightly incoherent singer who recommended a bottle of claret.
11. **Most songs cover…**
    **a. 1.5 octaves, that's comfortable for me.**
    Most songs cover around 1.5 octaves, whether they're classical, pop, rock, musical theatre or folk. A surprising number of respondents put 5 notes. To be honest, we racked our brains to think of a song that only uses 5 notes. Can anyone help us with suggestions?
    And to the handful of people who put 5 octaves into every song? Remember it's not how big it is…
12. **A professional voice user…**
    **b. Uses their voice for work more than 5 hours a day.**
    We weren't surprised to find over 80 people got this wrong. There is a myth that a professional voice user must be highly trained. Unfortunately for a lot of people who must use their voice for their job, this isn't always the case. Many people in this situation (sports coaches, clergymen, barristers, group leaders and teachers) have no formal vocal training.
    We created the 1 Minute Voice Warmup app to help people warm up and train their voice in seconds. Get it from the **Appstore** or **Google Play**

13. **Having a healthy voice means…**
    **b. You can express yourself clearly without getting a tired voice.**

*Congratulations if you got all 13 answers right.*

# MORE EAVESDROPPING ON COACHING SESSIONS

## MATCHING THE SONG TO THE CASTING

I had a new client coming for a consultation session. He is an actor comfortable with comedy and is often cast in comedy roles. He was looking for repertoire that would suit both his physical casting and his voice.

Having found out what sort of comedy types he would play (wry, dry, physical, quirky) I asked him to sing something he was already comfortable with. He chose "On the Street Where You Live" from *My Fair Lady*. He has a smooth, rich bass-baritone, which comes as somewhat of a surprise, as it doesn't really fit his physical casting. Watching him deliver the song, I am immediately struck by the fact that he is comfortable portraying physical extremes – his movements are clear, precise and definite. He is one of those actors who is physically funny to watch (think Rowan Atkinson or Charlie Chaplin).

My first thought (within 3 bars of him starting) was to give him the song "Funny" from *City of Angels*. The song is normally done as a type of rant by the leading man, but I thought we could make something interesting of it by taking it out of context. The client has the voice-type and range for the vocal writing, and his willingness to go towards extremes could be very useful.

In general, I felt keen to work with what are essentially standard songs, but to give them a twist that would fit his physical and comedy/pathos persona. I also came up with several alternative suggestions which could be used as well as, or instead of, the "Funny" song. I always suggest a classic-book type song, and in this case, Gershwin songs such as "They All Laughed" and "They Can't Take That Away From Me" came to mind. Sondheim songs include "Good Thing Going" from *Merrily We Roll Along*, and the highly unusual "Invocation and Instructions" from *The Frogs*. The latter is a complex (and long) front-cloth song telling the audience how to behave, and I thought that it would suit his quirky MC persona well (with a lot of judicious cutting).

Walking into an audition with songs that they know and that suit their casting and persona gives actors tremendous confidence, both in their ability as a performer and in the auditioning process.

### ***Learn a Song in 15 Minutes***

During the new client's session (see previous section) we worked on "Funny". I took him through the whole "Learn a Song in 15 Minutes" routine – it appears in the *Successful Singing Auditions* book and I describe it below.

1. Read the words as a script
2. Read the words in rhythm
3. Hum the tune without the words
4. "Miren" the words (see below)
5. Putting it together

Reading the words as text does not normally hold any mysteries for an actor, but it is astonishing how few actors read the words of a song "out of context" away from the music. Many are seduced or alarmed by the singing aspect of a song, so forget to use their current skills on the material. Reading the words as a script gives you the context, the flavour, the character and their "take" and helps you make decisions about what you want the song to do.

Reading the words in rhythm is an interesting one. Even with actors who read music (and many don't), it is rare to find someone who reads EXACTLY what's on the page. As an accomplished sight-reader and accompanist, it's what I've done for a living for a lonnnnng time, so it's really "second nature to me now" (a round of applause if you can name the song that contains that line – answer at the end). The purpose of reading the text in the rhythm of the song is to discover what changes to the natural speech cadences of the text the composer has made. Watch out for long words, stresses on weak syllables, diphthongs, and when normally short vowels are attached to long notes. The only way you can do this is to speak the words in exactly the rhythm that is written, including holding all the long notes for their correct values, even if it sounds odd!

Humming or sirening the melody is the next stage, and for this I prefer ng to mm, because it keeps the lips open and flexible (you'll see why in the next stage). I prefer the client to slide around between the pitches, rather than moving cleanly from one note to the other, because it seems to train the voice to negotiate the leaps in pitch more accurately. Also it is best to keep the *ng* sound small – it's not singing, so think of it as sirening quietly to yourself.

The next one confused my client temporarily – it's "mirening". This is sirening (humming) the melody while mouthing the words using the front of the tongue, lips and teeth. The *ng* sound is continuous, but the lips teeth and tongue can still make all the movements necessary for the consonants and vowels in the text. When clients first try this out, the temptation is to keep the mouth as still as possible, meaning that the bilabial consonants (m, b, p, etc) simply don't happen. This just means that you have not yet isolated the separate areas of the articulating mechanism. The point here is to practise the articulation, on the pitch the note happens, without worrying about "tone".

And finally, we put it all together. As the client pointed out, by this time, most of the words and the melody structure will have started to go into the memory anyway, even though, from my point of view, learning and memorizing are different things. One thing that does become clear having finished the process is how few errors you are likely to make in memorizing. Anything that might be a problem – complex words, strange rhythms or difficult pitch leaps, have all been dealt with in the separate stages of the learning process. With a short song, it is perfectly possible to complete the process in less than 15 minutes.

The client was able to sing the song accurately by the end of the session, and I have left him to go through anything that feels uncomfortable, ready for the next time.

*Incidentally, the quote comes from "I've Grown Accustomed to Her Face" from* My Fair Lady.

*  *  *

## "A HUNGRY YEARNING BURNING"

One of my West End clients arrived for an emergency two-hour session recently.

She had been invited to audition for not one but two film musical revivals. She needed two songs, ballad and up-tempo, suitable for the 40s–60s era. We needed two songs that we could use for both auditions.

We started with my standby composers for classic book musicals – Gershwin, Cole Porter and Irving Berlin. The Cole Porter songbook seemed to fit the best, and having tried out 8 bars of a few different songs, we settled on "Night and Day". It's a great tune, with a sweeping melody that descends an octave down to (in this key) low G. The casting brief said low voice, so that's what we went for. The song is quite easy to learn, and the patterns (albeit chromatic) repeat through the chorus. Even though the song is an up-tempo song (the accompaniment tells you that), the feel is that of a ballad, since the melody line moves slowly and smoothly. It's a useful song because of that.

We decided for this show that we didn't need the verse. It's an unusual decision for me, as normally in this style of music, the verse sets the scene (fact), and the chorus contains the emotion (feeling), and I like to include both. With many of these "standards", the verse is not well known, so the chorus when it arrives comes as a welcome surprise. In this case, the role she has been invited to audition for has songs that are like the writing of this chorus, so it seemed better to omit the verse.

Since the style of singing in this particular show can be slightly exaggerated, we played with singing the song "straight" and then à-la Shirley Bassey, complete with back-phrasing (delaying key words), forward-phrasing (bringing key words in ahead of the beat) and any other phrasing we could think of. Going to extremes often brings a performance to life, even if you wouldn't dream of performing it like that.

We then brought the song back to "normal" but kept the feel and fluidity of the exaggerated version. This seemed to fit the character's slightly heightened flavour. The client was happy with the song and the style, so we moved on to the second song…

### ***"My Chickens Just Ooze"***

The second song proved a little more difficult to find.

We were looking for something that was a little more character-based (rather than lyrical), so after discarding several songs (and composers) I suddenly thought of Bernstein, and his Broadway period. "I Can Cook Too" comes from *On The Town* and is a tour-de-force for a character actress.

I have played this song for only two others but thought it would fit this client extremely well. I played and sang a few bars and I could see she was excited by the prospect of learning the song. It's *very* wordy, but it is based around only a few musical patterns. This makes it easy to learn, if not to memorize!

We started with what I think of as the main section. This client picks things up very quickly, and it took only about 10 minutes to teach her all the patterns and their small variations. We did a stagger through to check progress, and she was 90% note perfect. Incidentally, I use the stagger through in much the same way as a theatre director uses it in rehearsal. You have done the movement blocking and learned the lines, but things are very much "work in progress". The stagger through gives you a rough idea of the shape and size of the piece, and the areas that need either checking or serious work.

I knew that my client would be dedicated in her learning at home, so we moved on to the characterization and voice qualities. In this case, the piece in the key we were working sits up around middle B (a seventh above middle C) and needs a slightly higher larynx position than my client was giving.

I worked with her on the possible speaking voice and patterns of the character, and we started with a young New Yorker, ditzy and blond to get the high energy and vocal height. We then made her slightly older and more "brunette" but keeping the high energy and presence. Using the characteristics of a speaking voice / dialect / vocal fingerprint helps in getting an actor into a different singing mode.

We also played with the idea of flipping into falsetto on certain notes or words. This client's background is classical-type training, which tends to focus on the beauty of sound and line. She is now starting to get excited by the idea that sound is only one part of the musical theatre equation. It can be much more fun to experiment with dramatic characteristics and different, even "unattractive" sounds, if they serve the text and drama.

This song will work well, for both auditions and for her song portfolio. She is coming back on Monday for a "wash and brush up" before the auditions (they're both on the same day). This is a client that I feel can cope with new songs for auditions – but I can't say I would recommend it for everyone!

*Just in case you're worried, the title I used here is one of the lines in the song.*

* * *

## *LORD OF THE RINGS* EPISODE 1

I'd like to share details of a coaching session from several years ago. This was a new client who has a *Lord of the Rings* audition in a week or so. He came to brush up on his singing technique and to ask about repertoire. He already has a song that he was comfortable with, so the first task is to find a suitable second song, both for him and for the casting. An experienced actor but not an experienced singer, it's important to find a piece that was easy to learn and also appropriate for the task in hand.

I wanted something folky yet powerful – he is a physical actor and needs to connect emotionally with the text. I suggested the song "Brother, My Brother" from the opening of the show *The Civil War*, by Frank Wildhorn. Wildhorn has a knack of writing simple, strong ballads with a powerful message.

If you've read the *Successful Singing Auditions* book, you will know that Gillyanne and I use the "Learn a song in 15 minutes" routine (see above). This works even for non-reading actors, although it might add another 5 minutes onto the time as I demonstrate the rhythm of each phrase. It is such a useful process, and actors often feel that spending this focused time at the beginning of the learning process helps them to feel more confident in both the song and their own ability.

In "Brother, My Brother" there are a few small phrases that are slightly awkward, but there is nothing untoward, and it is easy to latch onto the musical patterns that occur. It is quite extraordinary watching an actor move from struggling with the concept and shape of a song to understanding it in a few minutes. This client is sensible – he knows that he can practise at home but has also booked an extra session with me in a couple of days' time.

## *LORD OF THE RINGS* EPISODE 2

On Monday I took my client through the Learn a Song in 15 Minutes routine with his new song. On Wednesday he came back for another session, and the difference was extraordinary. Not only has he learned the song, and can sing it competently with a pianist, his voice sounds more secure, and he is displaying much more confidence in his own ability. He also commented that he had never been so far on in the song-learning process in such a short space of time. I know that many people simply don't believe that they can learn a song in 15 minutes, but the sequence works!

It is interesting to note that the new song sounds better than his original song. Now with him having spent the time at home getting to grips with the words, rhythm and melody using the process, we could spend our time concentrating on plot, subtext and characterization.

This song, "Brother, My Brother", is sung to a group of fellow soldiers in the show. For the LotR audition we decided to create a complete physical landscape for the character to inhabit. So, the singer becomes a sergeant in a scratch army – with the sentiments he conveys he couldn't really be a much higher rank. It's dusk, and the fires are being lit, with the camp settling down for the evening. The sergeant is surrounded by about 12 men – an intimate group within a larger encampment.

It is important for this client to fill in as much detail as possible in this way. It makes the portrayal of the song much easier and gives him something to concentrate on other than the sound he is making. This was essentially a rush job with a deadline, but my feeling is that having got through the first round he will come for more general technical input and access to a wider repertoire. He also has a bigger, more expansive voice but not yet the technique to sustain it, and I'm itching to help him discover it! He's coming again on Friday for a wash and brush up – I'll keep you posted

## *LORD OF THE RINGS* EPISODE 3

Back for the final session before the audition. *The Civil War* song is working much better and the subtext seems to have made a difference.

We work on playing the song today, and particularly on placing the various people and things mentioned in the text. It is amazing how powerful an actor's eyeline can be (that's the direction he looks in, not the black pencil). By placing characters around you, the audience can pick up subtle cues about your relationship with other people. It is possible to people the entire stage with relationships and still keep the story clear and focused. It is also important that wherever you place your other characters, that they act "naturally".

We work on keeping them in the same areas relative to each other, so that the audience is able to differentiate between, say, the band of soldiers that you fight with, and your best mates (who are part of the group but also closer to you). God is an interesting one – it is easy to put God up above you, but it's not always relevant to have him there. Of course, your characters can move around the stage, but you need to "follow" them with your eyeline or at the very least make the audience aware that you are still referring to the same person.

My other area of fascination is timeline. Since the song deals with past, present and future, real and idealized, I asked the client to decide where the future lay. Each client's personal timeline directions can be different, and it is good to start with what you do instinctively. In my case, my future tends to be streaming off forward and right, with the past streaming back to my left, almost touching my right shoulder. Different people can have lines moving forward/back, diagonal, up/down. Notice when you think about the future or the past, which way your mind's eye goes.

In this case his future was downstage and slightly to the right. (Incidentally this was good for staring off into the distance while facing out, which was handy!). It is then easy to introduce near future and distant future, or real future and wishful future, and put these into the song journey. The singer can refer to the future while communicating with someone, or just get "lost" in the future. I usually find that once these areas or ideas are embedded, the acting becomes much more detailed, more subtle, and strangely, more natural and more understandable. All of this comes from the text – I tend not to make it up!

With all of that in place, the song really took off, and the hair stood up on the back of my neck (no mean feat if you've seen my photo). Both he and I felt he was ready for the audition, and he was pleased to have two days to embed the information. Well, a couple of days later I had a phone call – he had managed the audition well and had been offered the recall.

* * *

## THE HILLS ARE ALIVE...

Another day, another audition coaching session.

> There's currently a lot of hype for a production of *The Sound of Music* in the West End. Andrew Lloyd Webber is on the lookout for a new unknown and is auditioning for unprofessional actresses to play Maria.

Yes, I know that's not true, but it makes a great line. (I believe the brief is an actress without full professional experience.) Anyway, two of my clients have had auditions for the role of Sister Berthe and needed advice on repertoire to take. The requirement was a Rodgers and Hammerstein song and an own choice piece.

For Sister Berthe we have a couple of pieces of information from the excellent Stage Agent website – she is the mistress of the novices, so we assume she has some ability with disciplining young people, and she is strict (well, that answers that one then). We are on the lookout for music that will suit a strict nun. Hmm.

Now I like taking music and giving it a slight tilt. With the first client I suggested the little-known piece from Cinderella – "The Stepsisters' Lament". Cinderella was one of the first musicals written for TV and is a Rodgers and Hammerstein piece. We played the song (which was originally a duet) as a solo for a strict teacher at a senior girls' school.

I set the scenario as standing for several minutes in the staff room listening to a group of teachers raving about a particular student. Having got impatient with them, she launches into the song pointing out that though the student may be good, clever, pretty and an all-round achiever, she is still irritating and doesn't deserve to win all the acclaim. This scenario gives enough of the vexed feeling without getting too strident, and keeping it in the appropriate age range of the character singing (40s and upwards) and the subject (late teens, early 20s).

## ...WITH THE SOUND OF NUNS

For the second client (who has a very different energy) I suggested something on a similar line but with a slightly different feel. This time we were going for the more restrained, nun-like qualities of the character. "Getting to Know You" was the song, (again a Rodgers and Hammerstein song) and the scenario we used was slightly different.

This time it was a teacher at a junior school on the first day of a new term. She walks in, writes "Getting to know you" on the blackboard as the topic of the morning. She is firm but kind. Unfortunately, there is one child ("George… don't do that") who is not able to concentrate on the message and who becomes gently disruptive. In this scenario, although the subject is much younger, the age of the singer can remain about the same (40s upwards) and the slightly gentler, more caring energy tempers the annoyance.

My clients usually find that getting a really focused subtext makes the song easier to sing, both vocally and performance-wise, and results in a number of specific targets to hit in the audition. It also makes the character easier to portray.

So much of the fear in auditions is due to not being focused on what you are doing, or not knowing what the job is in the first place. In a coaching session we might deal with what clothing or shoes the character is wearing, what the "set" is, how many people are on stage, in short, anything that makes the song journey clearer. These suggestions (and many others) are tools to get a good, workable performance in a difficult, stressful situation. Having a strong storyline to sit the song on gives a great deal of detail to the performance, and of course can be changed at will. The important thing for auditions is to make the choices in the first place.

* * *

The next section uncovers the techniques for finding new songs that fit, together with a done-for-you list of 120+ song suggestions for a song that breaks the fourth wall. Don't eat them all at once!

# THE SINGING AUDITION – CHOOSING REPERTOIRE

This is a short but vital section on choosing your songs. Here are some of the directions I use to reach the holy grail of musical theatre – the perfect audition song.

## FALLING OFF A LOG…

It seems that people are having so many problems finding repertoire to suit them. When I co-wrote the book *Successful Singing Auditions* with my wife Gillyanne Kayes, I created the FOAL Process (that's Falling off a Log to the uninitiated) to deal with this. I thought that having the structure of a book to write in was a good place to introduce a new process for choosing songs that suit you. I have to say that having created the process in 2000, I've been using it ever since for all sorts of different projects. I even found my brother several years' worth of birthday presents by running the FOAL Process on him! Finding the things that you do so easily (it's like falling off a log) can boost your career or even make you change your focus.

An interview with Hollywood actress Kari Wahlgren in the papers last week demonstrated this only too clearly. Kari had moved to Hollywood from a stage career in Kansas. She worked behind a desk, answered phones and taught in order to make ends meet. And she did auditions.

"I think I had a particularly rough on-camera audition, and I found myself thinking very negatively, and I didn't like how negative I was getting about the whole process – and about living in L.A. in general. And I thought, you know, I really have to change my attitude or I'm never gonna make it in this city. So I decided I would take a little break from on-camera auditions and just focus on my voice work."

She had found her FOAL area, and the work started flowing. Now most of her work is as a voiceover artist, with credits including "The Wild", "Super Robot Monkey", and the video game version of "From Russia With Love". All in all, her voice has featured in more than 100 animated films and video games. Having established herself in a comfortable area, she's more ready for those on-camera auditions.

"I think you have to get to a place where you enjoy the journey, because you have to audition so much, and there are so many things you don't get," she says. "You really have to enjoy the process."

Absolutely!

* * *

## CHOOSING YOUR SONG PORTFOLIO

I want to clarify what I consider to be the necessary contents of the song portfolio: six-to-nine songs that you can do immediately, in the right key (or keys) for you, that fit your casting, or that you have an excellent reason to sing.

They should contain the following:

1. A classic book song, or Gershwin/Porter/Kern standard for lyrical singing;
2. A contemporary drama song (*Les Misérables*, *Jekyll and Hyde*, *Wild Party* etc);
3. A pop song (pop, rock, R&B, gospel, anything going back as far as 1950s pop, in whatever style suits you best)
4. A standard with a simple accompaniment (for when you hear the pianist can't play!)
5. (6, 7, 8, 9) Own choice songs, chosen to show your strengths. In other words, if you sing contemporary drama well, add another one to the list. If you sing Dusty Springfield well, add that. If you sing heart-on-sleeve songs, add one of those. If you do power ballads, add another one of those. Anything that you do easily and well.

Even within those first four categories, there are several options. If you really aren't a ballad singer (and for some character actors a straight ballad really doesn't fit their casting), then find a story song or a patter song of that period (theatre songs from the 1920s–1960s). The feel is more classic even if the song is for a character. Cole Porter's "Tale of the Oyster" or "The Physician", even Gilbert and Sullivan patter songs come under this category.

But beware of updates – "The Sun Who's Rays" from *The Mikado* (G&S) would fit, but "The Sun Who's Rays" from *The Hot Mikado* wouldn't (even though it's essentially the same show), because the feel has been changed to R&B / gospel / pop.

* * *

## TOP 60 HOUSE NUMBERS FOR MEN TO SING

You're a musicals singer looking for a song that can reach out to an audience, one that you can play to them directly. You're looking for a "House number".

A House number is a song that crosses the invisible fourth wall between the actor and the audience, the wall that exists in the character's mind (after all, in most plays and musicals the characters don't know they're being watched by a group of people).

In musical theatre there are only a few true House numbers, but you can make other songs cross the fourth wall fairly easily.

Here are the top 60 House numbers for men that can be sung to the audience directly, followed by 60 House numbers for women. In each list I've sorted the songs into three categories:

- the true House number
- the audience number
- the soliloquy.

**The first category is the true House number:** The singer is fully aware that the audience is there and "comes out" of the show.

"If You Want To Die In Bed", and "American Dream" from *Miss Saigon*, and "Oh What A Circus" from *Evita* are good examples of the true House number. Sondheim writes great House numbers, including "Comedy Tonight" and "Everybody Ought To Have A Maid" from *A Funny Thing Happened on the Way to the Forum*, and "Invocation to the Gods And Instructions to the Audience" from the rarely performed *The Frogs* (it takes place in a swimming pool).

**In the second category**, the character plays to an audience on stage as part of the show. The most obvious song for the men is "Master of the House" from *Les Misérables*. The MC from *Cabaret* usually expands the Berlin nightclub audience to include the actual theatre audience with songs such as "Wilkommen" and "If You Could See Her". In *Barnum*, "The Museum Song" is sung to a general group of people, as is "Bigger Isn't Better". "Springtime for Hitler" is sung to the audience in *The Producers*, as is "Beautiful Girls" (from *Follies*).

Consider the songs "Use What You Got" from *The Life*, "Pinball Wizard" from *Tommy*, and "I Am What I Am" from *La Cage Aux Folles*. "Stand Up And Fight" from *Carmen Jones*, and "Get Me To The Church On Time" from *My Fair Lady* can be house numbers. You could also get away with "All I Care About Is Love", and "Mr Cellophane", from *Chicago*. An unusual one is "Come Up To My Office" from *Parade*, where the leading man "re-enacts" a scene in a courtroom, according to the imaginary version of his young female co-workers.

Tribute Musicals are a useful source of House numbers such as "That'll Be The Day" and "Johnny Be Good" from *Buddy*, or "I Want To Break Free" from *We Will Rock You.* Virtually any song from *Hedwig And The Angry Inch* would work, including "Sugar Daddy" and "Angry Inch". *The 25th Annual Putnam County Spelling Bee* has an implied audience for the spelling contest, and the "children" sing songs such as "My Unfortunate Erection" straight to them. "I Can Do That" (from *A Chorus Line*) is sung to Zach who is actually seated at the back of the real audience.

**Then there's the third type** – the unifocus song (the soliloquy) that has an outward feel, or asks questions, or contains rhetoric. "Funny" from *City of Angels.* "What Is It About Her" from *Wild Party*, and "Don't Take Much" from *The Life* work well. "All I Need Is The Girl" from *Gypsy* will work, as will "Tonight At Eight" and "She Loves Me" from *She Loves Me.* Check out "How To Handle A Woman" from *Camelot*, "Being Alive" from *Company*, and two from *Parade* ("Pretty Music", and "Big News").

Oddly enough, "Anthem" from *Chess* could work as a fourth wall number as the Russian could be sharing his story with the audience. You might also experiment with songs like "Make Them Hear You" from *Ragtime*, "If I Were A Rich Man" from *Fiddler on the Roof*, or "Thank Heaven For Little Girls" from *Gigi.* And two to include in this list are "And They're Off" from *A New Brain*, and "Dressing Them Up" from *Kiss of the Spider Woman.*

"Giants In The Sky" from *Into The Woods*, "Larger Than Life" from *My Favorite Year*, "Corner Of The Sky" from *Pippin* and "Guys and Dolls" (the title song) will translate well across the fourth wall. And from *Les Misérables*, you might explore "Dog Eat Dog" – Thénadier's great solo scene from Act 2, or try "King Of The World" (*Songs for a New World*). Then there's "Dentist!" from *Little Shop of Horrors*, "Leaning On A Lamppost" from *Me and My Girl*, and "Reviewing the Situation" from *Oliver!*

You can raid pretty much any revue-style show for material – Sondheim's shows are a very good place to start – "The Ballad of

Booth" from *Assassins*, "Everybody Says Don't" from *Anyone Can Whistle*, or "These Are My Friends" from *Sweeney Todd*, sung as Todd is reunited with his razors.

Incidentally, "The Soliloquy" from *Carousel* won't work, because the singer is arguing with himself and is definitely not including anyone else except perhaps God. However, "This Is The Moment" can work because you can share your success with the audience.

Slower songs don't tend to work but there are exceptions: "What More Can I Say" from *Falsettos*, or "Higher Than A Hawk" from *Calamity Jane*. "A Little Happiness" from *Personals* is a more reflective story that is designed to be shared with the audience.

Remember, that House numbers are designed to communicate directly with the audience, so make sure you include plenty of eye contact in your performances. Enjoy!

## TOP 60 HOUSE NUMBERS FOR WOMEN FROM MUSICALS

If you're looking for songs for women that you can use to communicate directly with an audience,here are 60 house numbers for women that can be sung to the audience directly. Once again, I've listed the songs in three categories:

- the true House number
- the audience number
- the soliloquy

**The first category is the true house number:** The singer is fully aware that the audience is there and "comes out" of the show.

"Diva's Lament" from *Spamalot*, of course, "You Can Always Count On Me" from *City of Angels*, and "When You're Good To Mama" from *Chicago* spring to mind immediately. Other true house numbers include "Big Spender" from *Sweet Charity* (originally a chorus number but can be sung by one person), "I Just Wanna Dance" from *Jerry Springer*, "Jonny One Note" from *Babes in Arms*, and "Nobody Does It Like Me" – the Cy Coleman song from the musical *SeeSaw*. And "Miss Byrd" from *Closer Than Ever* shares her secret across the fourth wall.

Many of the songs from the Victorian Music Hall era work as house numbers including "Waiting At the Church", "If It Wasn't For the 'Ouses In Between", and even ballads such as "The Boy I Love Is Up In The Gallery". Then there are the songs written in a musicals style such as "Girl in 14G", and "The Alto's Lament".

**In the second category**, the character plays to an audience on stage as part of the show. "Good and Evil" from *Jekyll and Hyde* is a great example as Lucy sings to the "audience" in the pub. Then there's "Don't Cry For Me Argentina" (*Evita*), "I Speak Six Languages" from *The 25th Annual Putnam County Spelling Bee*, "Beat Out Dat Rhythm" from *Carmen Jones*, "Man Wanted" from *Copacabana*, and "Blow Gabriel Blow" from *Anything Goes.* "I'm Still Here" from *Follies*, "Broadway Baby" from *Follies* have the actors deliberately sing to their colleagues on the stage. "The Saga Of Jenny" from *Lady in the Dark* is sung in a courtroom, and you might just get away with "Life of the Party" from *Wild Party*.

**Then there's the third type** – the unifocus song (the soliloquy) that has an outward feel, or asks questions, or contains rhetoric. Probably the most famous song is "I Cain't Say No" from *Oklahoma.* Then there's "I'm Shy" from *Once Upon A Mattress*, "Everybody Says Don't", and "There Won't Be Trumpets", from *Anyone Can Whistle*, and "I'm A Stranger Here Myself" from *One Touch of Venus.*

Check out Holding To The Ground from *Falsettos*, My Brother Lived In San Francisco from *Elegies for Angels Punks and Raging Queens*, "I Hate Men" from *Kiss Me Kate*, and "My Strongest Suit" from *Aida.*

For the more old-fashioned amongst you, there's "I Think I May Want To Remember Today" from *Starting Here, Starting Now*, "Tale of the Oyster" (*Fifty Million Frenchmen*), and "The Physician" (*Nymph Errant*).

You might get away with a strong story song such as "Waiting For The Music To Begin" (*Witches of Eastwick*) if you set out to tell the audience members the story. And of course, there's "Nothing" (*A Chorus Line*) where the entire song is sung to Zach, who sits in the audience during the show. It's therefore very easy to turn it into a house number and address the audience directly and individually.

Other songs include "Gimme Gimme" from *Thoroughly Modern Millie*, "I Know Things Now" from *Into the Woods*, "Defying Gravity" from

*Wicked*, and "Always The Bridesmaid" from *I Love You, You're Perfect, Now Change.*

Back to Sondheim again for "The Ladies Who Lunch" from *Company*, "The Story of Lucy and Jessie" (from certain productions of *Follies*), and "Can That Boy Foxtrot" (a duet that can be sung as a solo) from *Marry Me A Little*, or cut from *Follies*, depending on who you read.

Then there's "Everybody's Girl" from *Steel Pier*, "Old Fashioned Love Story" from *Wild Party*, "When You Got It, Flaunt It" from *The Producers*, and "How Did I End Up Here" from *Romance Romance.* You might consider "One Hundred Easy Ways" from *Wonderful Town*, or "My New Philosophy" from *You're A Good Man Charlie Brown*, and experiment with a song like "Cockeyed Optimist" from *South Pacific.*

You can raid the revue-style musicals such as *Closer Than Ever* for songs like "Back On Base", or "The Bear, The Tiger, The Hamster and The Mole", and *Songs for a New World* for "I'm Not Afraid Of Anything". You can also do what the musicals are doing currently and raid the pop/disco/rock scene for suitable songs – "Holding Out For A Hero" started as a Bonnie Tyler song but is now in both *Footloose* and *Shrek II.*

It is unusual for a slower song to work as a house number, but here are a few exceptions:

"Maybe I Like It This Way" from *Wild Party*, "That's Him" from *One Touch Of Venus*, "Why Him" from *Carmelina*, "Bill" (from *Oh Lady! Lady!* and versions of *Showboat*) and of course, "Funny Girl" from *Funny Girl.*

Remember that a House number is sung directly to the audience, so make sure you have plenty of eye contact!

* * *

## "I NEED A POP SONG…"

I will often get clients coming to me saying that they need "a pop song" for their portfolio. An increasing number of musicals are being written with music based in the contemporary commercial music styles. However, I usually find that in the student's minds, "pop" means only one thing – Britney or Kylie. In the context of musical theatre training, pop has a much bigger meaning.

You wouldn't take the same song to *Mamma Mia!* and to *Rent*, because the writing, the drama and the musical style is so different. It is normal for an actor to have resonances with certain styles, and it is this that can support the choice of song in this category.

If you are a comfortable improvisor with dramatic flair, look to the gospel and R&B canon. If you have a more lyric voice (and a sweeter disposition) look further back to the 40s and 50s and the Easy Listening canon. If you are good with storytelling, there are hundreds of commercial recordings of story or situation songs.

Listen out for singers whose performances or sound you admire and check out their back catalogue – you may be surprised at what they have recorded. There are thousands of examples of potential audition songs to choose from – although some of them may need a little lateral thinking – Cilla Black and Cliff Richard (both recording artists spanning many years) have recorded some great story songs, even if their singing styles are not necessarily considered acceptable today. Take away their performance and revisit the songs, and you have some good potential audition material. We are now seeing pop legends having musicals created around their back catalogue – Billy Joel is one recent example.

The "pop" musical is here to stay, so it's important for performers to discover which categories of contemporary commercial music are going to work for them.

## "I NEED A COMEDY SONG…"

I also get students who say, "I must have a comedy song". My first question is "why?"

If you are a comedy specialist, you have usually already found several suitable songs. But not everyone plays comedy well, so do you really need one?

My second question is "what type of comedy?". A chunk of the FOAL Process is devoted to your tastes in comedy – stand-up and situation, likes and dislikes. There are almost as many types of comedy as there are types of musical style. Do you prefer clever word-play (*I'm Sorry I Haven't A Clue*) and puns (*I'm Sorry I'll Read That Again*), slapstick (a long line of performers from Buster Keaton to Mr Bean), surreal (Eddie Izzard, The League of Gentlemen), motor-mouth (Robin Williams, Richard Pryor), "real-life" (*The Office*, *Marion and Geoff*)? Whatever you prefer, there will be a set of songs that will fit your tastes.

Comedy is also a state of mind. The unexpected and the unusual, or the juxtaposition of two different and opposing ideas can be funny by their very nature. Reworking the subtext of a song is an excellent way of portraying a particular comedy style. Off the top of my head, Barbra Streisand on film (His Love Makes Me Beautiful), and Spike Jones and the City Slickers on record ("You Always Hurt The One You Love") have reworked songs to bring out the comedy. If you are looking for a comedy song for your portfolio, work out your brands of comedy first and then start looking for the material to fit! Or you could book a coaching session with me, of course…

www.DrGillyanneKayesJeremyFisherInspirationSession.as.me

* * *

The next section goes into much more detail about the targeted techniques I use when my singers arrive with problems. This is the meat-and-potatoes of vocal troubleshooting, the specific tips, hacks and techniques that I use regularly to help my singers get the recalls and the jobs. Enjoy.

# TOP VOCAL TECHNIQUES AND TIPS

The look of this book came from this beautiful photo, so serious and yet so bizarre, it made me laugh the moment I saw it.

Here is a miscellany of stories, techniques and examples, written for different magazines, blogs and website over the years. My style morphs slightly for each different platform but the value of the information remains the same. Let me know your favourites!

## EASY TOP NOTES – HOW TO STRETCH YOUR VOICE

Today I'm focusing on finding easy top notes in a young male voice.

Interesting lesson today with a young singer songwriter about to go to LA on contract. He's 19, writing good material, and his voice wasn't doing quite what he wanted from his writing. Could I help?

We had a single Skype vocal coaching session the day before he flew out. He'd sent me a YouTube video of one of his songs, and I could hear that he wasn't completely comfortable. He did not have easy top notes.

The issue (and he didn't realize this himself) was that he was writing songs and particularly choruses that sat right on his gear change. The chorus we were working on sat up on E above middle C. Now that isn't particularly high for a man's voice, but it IS high if your writing stays there all the time. The human voice doesn't work well when it must sing a repeated phrase around a gear change or break with no let-up. The more he sang it, the more tired he got. We had to fix it and fast.

### *Where Is Your Vocal Gear Change?*

The first thing I needed to check was exactly where his natural vocal break was. Male voices don't finish settling until up to 27 years old, so it was possible he was still developing. I used sliding fifths up and down in semitones from the middle of his range until we hit the voice "crack point" into his falsetto. He very sensibly asked me if I wanted him to be active in preventing the crack or not, so we did both versions: allowing the crack to happen & working actively to avoid it.

It was where I thought it might be – around Eb above middle C – and I suspect that his voice is still settling. But the interesting part of the exercise came when he showed me how he actively worked to avoid it. He was keeping the "texture" and thickness of the vocal folds the same, maintaining the volume, and pushing with his abdominal wall for strength. This was making his throat close – his false vocal folds were tightening and coming in to "help" and were making his voice tight. This was making him vocally tired.

Now there are two things you can do – temporary and permanent. The temporary thing is to lower the key slightly so he can stay in his comfortable range most of the time. The permanent thing is slightly more complex but would allow him to write wherever he wanted in his voice.

He had to learn to stretch his vocal folds.

### *Stretching Your Vocal Folds*

Stretched vocal folds can vibrate faster. And vocal folds vibrating faster means you can go higher in your range.

If you want an active chest voice sound (as opposed to a falsetto-based sound) you NEED to know how to stretch and thin your vocal folds and stay in a chest-voice mix. It's quite normal for a young guy not to know how to sing higher. During adolescence the vocal folds grow exponentially, and in a very short space of time you end up with something much bigger and thicker than you're used to, which can be difficult to manoeuvre (stop sniggering at the back).

So how do you learn to stretch your vocal folds in one Skype vocal coaching session? Here's how I did it.

I asked him to speak the lyrics to find out where his normal speaking voice sat (around the A a tenth below middle C). Then I showed him how to speak the lyrics using a loud-moaning-type sound. Loud moaning helps the vocal folds to stretch while staying relatively thick. This sounds ridiculous the first time you do it, but there's a good reason for sticking with the instruction. That slight stretch means they will sit more comfortably on a higher pitch without too much extra effort.

Then I got him to speak slightly higher while keeping the moany setup, and moved his speaking voice pitch higher while still staying in that moany chest voice mix. Within seconds he was speaking up on the pitches he was writing. Then when I then got him to play guitar and sing the lyrics with the same moany chest mix, he went straight to the right sound at the right pitch and couldn't believe how easy it was.

After only a few minutes he was finding his easy top notes quickly and without any extra effort. He was accessing a much more flexible voice.

### *Rebalancing Your Voice and Breathing*

The next thing was to "rebalance" his voice to accommodate the more flexible vocal folds.

Before, he'd been using abdominal strength and breath force to blast his way up, so we need to rework his breathing slightly. Stretched vocal folds need less air to vibrate well. If you think about it, that makes sense – a big bulky structure is going to need a stronger airflow to make it move than a thinner structure. I reminded him to keep the moany chest voice mix and told him to back off the air pressure slightly.

Immediately his voice sounded as if it had just shifted up a third, and the previously difficult high chorus wasn't difficult and didn't even sound as high as before. Instant easy top notes!

Now he's happy flying off to meetings and songwriting sessions tomorrow, and he knows that he can Skype me for an online vocal technique lesson any time from LA.

Job done.

* * *

## CHECK YOUR VOWELS

I'm in London giving coaching sessions, and today turned out to be dodgy vowels day.

Three clients were having problems sustaining notes clearly. For all of them, the notes weren't unusually high in their range but there was a slight instability that was feeling uncomfortable and making the sound shake a little. Since every other part of their range was sounding clean and solid, I started listening really closely to the vowels they were singing.

Let me give you an example: One client was singing "Stars". So the long notes include the following: Grace, Face, Flame, Night, Light, Sky, Aim, Same, Flames, (door)Way, Paradise, Price.

*Notice Anything?*

Every one of the above words has a diphthong. And with all three singers that day, I heard something that I hear unfortunately far too often. A hybrid single vowel instead of the dual-vowel diphthong.

Grace would become a sort of Australian Gress (or a hybrid halfway between gress and greese). And Light became a cross between lawt and lit).

These singers (and many others) don't know how to deal with diphthongs, either the timing or the actual vowels you're supposed to sing.

So here are the diphthong rules (which of course are made to be broken…)

1. Work out phonetically which vowels you're supposed to sing. Sing them.
2. Work out the timing of each vowel so that it fits the word, the music style, the dramatic moment and your voice.

Let's break each one down a bit more.

The two vowel sounds in the diphthong in "Light" in RP is ah-ih, or the vowels in cat and kit. This might come as a surprise if you think it should be Lah-eet. Now of course there's room for negotiation here, depending on how your character normally speaks. Did I mention that your character should be singing in the same dialect or accent that (s)he speaks? I've never understood how some cowboys in Oklahoma have had the time to have classical singing lessons…

So if your character is from the Deep South, you might sing Laht and miss out the second vowel sound completely (also useful for Gospel).

Whatever you decide your two vowels are, do experiment with singing both of them. For my client singing the *Les Misérables* piece, we changed his vowel shapes in "Light" to Ah as in Cat, and the ih as in Kit. "Flame" became Flem with the tiniest ih (kit) at the end. (Incidentally, I believe falling into Phlegm could be classed by Dante as the sixth circle of hell.)

Which brings us to timing. This is very much dependent on the style of the piece you're singing (and whether you want to stay with the style or change it).

Given that you have two different vowel sounds in a diphthong, you can decide when you're going to move, and how fast.

Classical singing relies on staying on the first vowel as long as possible, then moving very quickly to the second vowel right at the end of the note value. Sometimes the second vowel is missed out entirely, sometimes a hybrid single vowel is sung instead.

Then you have the opposite – sing the first vowel quickly then move very fast onto the second vowel and hold it. Used more in pop and some contemporary musical theatre, and useful for character work.

And you have a third, which is the slow transition. You start on the first vowel, then move the tongue, jaw and lips very slowly towards the second vowel. Frank Sinatra was the past master at this. It gives a lot of colour to the word, highlights the meaning rather than the sound of your voice, and is very useful indeed in musical theatre. There are variations on this theme – hold the first vowel a little longer and then slow-transition until just before the end of the note, or slow-transition to arrive on the second vowel two-thirds of the way through.

Back to "Stars". Javert, the character who sings this, is old-fashioned, straightlaced and very rule-bound. We decided his "singing sound" was probably in the more classical, semi-operatic mould as that gives a feeling of formality. With so many long notes in his piece (the end of almost every phrase) we focused mainly on the more classical timing: staying on the first vowel as long as possible and popping the second vowel in just before the note finishes. Lahhhhhhhh-iht and Flehhhhhhhhh-ihm. So far, so peachy.

But we did decide to make two exceptions because it seemed to work best with that singer and that point in the song: On the doorWAY to Paradise. On the word Way, we put in a quite extreme timing change – very short on the first vowel and straight onto the second: Weh-ihhhhhh.

And for the word pay the PRICE, we added a slow transition from one vowel to the next: prahh-a-eh-e-ih-ih-ihce (that one is difficult to write but easy to do).

Quite apart from sounding better, more stylistically accurate and easier to understand, something extra happened for my client. The resonance improved and his voice became much more stable throughout.

So if you hit a little instability in your long notes sometimes, check your vowels!

* * *

## FROM GROANERS TO *GLEE* – TO Bb OR NOT TO Bb

Why do some people find it difficult to pitch notes?

What's happening when people sing out of tune?

Let's break down the question of tuning and start with what "pitch" means.

### *Pitch*

Pitch as we think of it is a regular oscillation of airwaves. If the airwaves are oscillating at 220 times per second, we hear the A below middle C (A3). If the airwaves oscillate at 440 times per second, we hear the A above middle C (A4). Each doubling of the oscillations creates a note one octave higher (880=A5, etc). It doesn't matter what causes the oscillations (guitar string, vocal folds, ruler on the desk…), if the vibrations are regular, we'll hear it as a pitch.

When we're learning about pitch as children, we need to be able to distinguish different pitches we hear and apply those pitches to our own voice. This requires an awareness of pitch direction, the recognition of broad melodic patterns and shapes, awareness of their own personal voice and vocal range, and a process to find the notes.

### *Tuning (Matching Pitch)*

What we think of as tuning is in reality a form of matching pitch. Children go through four stages of pitch matching to sing in tune. The difficulty lies when a child gets stuck in one stage and doesn't progress, even in adulthood. Here's a description of the four stages of pitch matching that children go through, taken from Gillyanne Kayes' introduction in the *Singing Express* series.

**Phase 1:** Words rather than melody are the centre of interest; singing is likely to be chant-like with a restricted pitch range; falling melodic patterns occur more often.

**Phase 2:** Developing awareness and conscious control of pitch; able to follow larger melodic contours of a song; sense of musical "key" is phrase-based; vocal pitch range for song singing expands

**Phase 3:** Increased accuracy of melodic shape and intervals, but may change "key" whilst control of vocal range is still in development

**Phase 4:** No significant melodic or pitch errors when singing relatively simple songs of own culture
(Four stages of development, adapted from Welch 1998)

In the *Singing Express* series, we created several different exercises to help children progress through the stages of pitch matching, including:

- Gliding and landing
- Finding your note – stepping and jumping
- Finding your note – singing together

Gliding and landing is a great way to introduce the concept of moving and holding pitch. Allow the child to slide their voice around on any vowel or humming sound, then land on a pitch, either by stopping or holding one note. If possible, get the child to land on a note first, then match it yourself. This has two great effects – the child feels a sense of achievement when you match their sound so easily, and it also requires them to sustain sound for a little longer than in their speaking voice, to give you the chance to match it.

By the way, it's tricky for inexperienced singers to pitch match to a piano or a guitar. The timbre of both instruments is very different from a voice, and you may experience children latching on to a harmonic in the sound rather than the fundamental note. In all of the *Singing Express* video and audio demonstrations, we asked our adult performers to sing with minimal vibrato. Singing in a straighter tone helps children identify the note more easily.

### *Scale Patterns*

A word about scale patterns. Anyone who has studied classical music knows about scales (major, minor, diminished, etc). But most popular music is based on modes rather than classical scales. And almost all vocal riffing (very fast patterns of notes used extensively in pop / R&B) is based on modes. If your students have grown up with popular music and haven't had much exposure to classical music, the patterns of classical scales may confuse them. If you are going to use scale patterns as part of your singing, start with the pentatonic mode (it's usually pretty easy for people to learn).

### *Breathing and Pitching*

Let's talk breathing for singing. In order to maintain a pitch, you need to keep a stream of air constant. We don't normally use a constant stream of air while speaking – all those stopped consonants, voiced and unvoiced fricatives, and the normal speed of speech means it's not necessary. Sustaining a constant airflow for one extended pitch is an unusual act. Coupled with that, the lungs work as a dynamic system that overfills, decreases in size and ends up underfilled, causing you to take another breath (to overfill again). This means that you can be only halfway through a note but heading for negative air pressure already. Singing a single pitch is a complicated balance of vibration, air pressure and lung elasticity. If that's how complicated breathing can be, it's astounding that we sing at all!

### *Pitching Problems*

Assuming you have progressed through the four stages of pitch matching, and you have some ability to maintain breath pressure, what problems might you face?

Finding your start note. In order to find the starting note of a song or phrase, you must extrapolate from a heard sound where it lies in your voice. Even adult singers can find this a challenge. Any female choral conductor working with a male choir will tell you that they must alter their pitch range and vocal timbre to get the men to match the starting note they give.

Try this experiment. Record yourself singing a short melody, then play it back. Is it easier to pitch the first note when you're listening to your own voice? This tells you that we don't just listen for the number of vibrations per second, we're also listening to the timbre of the sound and the context of the note. Even if you have never listened to your recorded voice before, you can usually tell where in your pitch range the first note lies just by hearing your own voice making the note.

### *Resonance*

The word resonance is a wonderful catch-all for timbre, projection, depth, tone, beauty and quality. Your vocal tract is very flexible, partly due to the ability of the tongue, jaw and soft palate to swallow and chew. The voice is the only instrument that can change size, shape

AND texture while producing sound. By moving the surfaces inside your vocal tract, you can enhance or subdue different harmonics, causing changes of vowel/consonant, and changes of tone quality. This means that once you have set your vocal folds in motion with their regular vibrations (whatever pitch you want to sustain), you have a massive number of choices of space/shape in your upper vocal tract to play with.

And these resonance adjustments can cause you to sound "in tune" to your colleagues, or sound as if you are under or over the note. This depends on the context of the note, the habits of the person singing, and most important, the beliefs of the person listening. We've had many classical singing teachers on our training courses who say that a musical theatre speech quality sounds flat to them, because it doesn't have the same harmonic pattern as the timbres considered acceptable in classical singing.

Here's an experiment you can do with your singing groups.

1. Get the group to sing a note or chord on an EE vowel. Now get them to keep the feeling of the EE (so the tongue stays high and wide) and change vowel to an ER (a schwa). You'll get an ER with a flavour of EE. You're boosting the brighter harmonics inherent in an EE vowel.

2. Now get the group to do the opposite. Start with a standard AH vowel (the tongue is low in the mouth and slightly backed). Keep the low and backed tongue position and change the vowel to a schwa (ER). Now you'll get an ER with a flavour of AH. It's not the same ER you had in the first part of the exercise.

3. Now divide the group into two. One half will sing with the EE vowel flavour, and the other with the AH vowel flavour. Get them to sing a line of a song, stand back and listen to the tuning!

4. The fun really starts when you begin to allocate vowel tunings between the parts. We've used this successfully to change the sound of a choir in 60 seconds. For example, basses and altos tune to an AH, tenors and sopranos tune to an EE. Then reverse the choices. The sound of the chorus changes instantly.

You can see us working this exercise with a 100-strong choir on the Vocal Process YouTube channel.

The great thing about this exercise is that you get to choose which tuning you prefer, since none of them are "wrong", they're just personal choice. Also, some tuning combinations are better for certain styles of music. Musical theatre tends to prefer an EE or ER tuning since clarity of text is important, whereas classical romantic music tends to prefer an AH or even AW tuning since warmth and roundness of sound is important.

In your own singing, if you find that you occasionally sing out of tune, or there's a particular note or phrase that bugs you, try altering your underlying vowel tuning for that phrase and see/hear/feel if it makes a difference. You might surprise yourself!

Which brings us to *Glee*. This television series has highlighted one major change in taste concerning singing and music perception: **Autotune.** Every song on *Glee* is autotuned to within an inch of its life, and young singers are now used to hearing and revering this unrealistic impression of singing. Ironically, since Autotune tends to remove a singer's personality, it seems clear that a voice's individuality is often revealed, and celebrated, by the slight mistunings or changes of resonance.

Think of your mistunings as being expressions of your personality and celebrate them!

*A version of this article first appeared in Music Teacher magazine under the title "From Groaners to Glee", and is reproduced here by kind permission of Rhinegold Publishing*

* * *

## BELLA SIGNORA, CLASSICAL SCALES AND OTHER ANOMALIES

I've been working with a lot of singing teachers in the past few months. They teach in as many genres as you can name. Most have a performing background. A few have performed exclusively in contemporary commercial music (CCM) genres, most have had some classical training and/or performed as classical singers. On our recent Singing Teacher Training in Australia, we did a spot poll on how many teachers in the room taught solely classical music.

The answer?

One.

In another of our presentations, we mentioned a piece of research by Dr Marisa Lee that highlighted music consumption: according to the Nielsen database, in the US list of vocal music recordings purchased in 2016, only 1% was classical. That means **99%** of the vocal music bought, listened to and aspired to is "non-classical" – CCM, rock, pop, gospel, easy listening, folk, jazz, world and all their myriad subdivisions.

So why, when we work with singing teachers, are we hearing classical scales and arpeggios in warmups? Is there still a belief that classical is best, classical is the only technique, classical is the basis of everything, everyone should be learning classical?

Even I suffered from "classical superiority" as a young professional. I went to a music college that did not appreciate non-classical music. It took me a long time to feel that if I worked in musical theatre I wasn't "wasting my talent".

The odd thing is, when pressed, most classical teachers will say it takes years to learn to sing classical music well. If I'm a 19-year-old country & western singer with a new recording contract, why am I learning to sing "O mio dolce ardor" when my producer is pressing me to record my new album? Can I not just learn the patterns and techniques that fit the genre I have chosen to work in and get to the studio?

### ***Let's Get Specific***

Let's talk using the classical scales and arpeggios in warmups. Classical scales based on the Ionian mode like the C major scale (C-D-E-F-G-A-B-C) and arpeggio (C-E-G-C-G-E-C) don't really occur in music that isn't classical. Pentatonic scale patterns occur. Other modes like the Dorian, yes. Jazz scales, yes. Leaps, yes. Slides, yes.

The question remains, why use classical scales and arpeggios with singers who are not singing classical music professionally?

The answer might be that the classical scale is so embedded in classical music that many teachers don't realize it's a classical scale at all. It's just the scale, right? Think of the vocal music of Rossini, Handel, Mozart, Bellini. Packed with scale patterns, both in straight form (Mozart's "Marten aller Arten") and twisting back on itself (Handel's "Rejoice Greatly"). Scale exercises are ideal for this type of music as you can embed the patterns of the song/aria in your warmup. The Vaccai exercises are stunning examples of 19th-century vocalizes that use the patterns of the (then) current music to create practice songs. And if I'm working with a soprano singing Rossini cadenzas, I will often use small sections of the cadenza pattern to create exercises – embedding the phrase/music shapes while we go.

So why aren't we doing the same with contemporary singers or musical theatre singers? Using the patterns that already exist in the music as warmups or skill-based exercises? Why go with classical scales and arpeggios, or (my pet hate) Bella Signora?

### *Bella Signora*

Oh yes, can we talk Bella Signora for a moment? It's a favourite of musical theatre MDs to end a warmup before a show. For those of you who have not come across it, the basic pattern with a couple of variations shown below.

Figure 1: Three versions of Bella Signora.

In its simplest form, Bella Signora is an arpeggio + a little turn + a straight scale downwards covering a ninth. Which is of course ideal for singing *School of Rock* or *Miss Saigon* or *Wicked* or *Spring Awakening.*

Not.

And it's in Italian. Can you name any musicals where the cast sings in Italian or with an Italian accent? I can only think of one – "Light In The Piazza". In *Phantom of the Opera*, Carlotta and Piangi sing with Italian accents, and Pirelli (*Sweeney Todd*) sings in cod-Italian for half his role but they are the only singers in each show to do so.

### *Vowel Shapes*

Ah, but the received wisdom is that Italian vowels are the best, the clearest, the most open. For classical singing, yes. But you don't use Italian vowels in *We Will Rock You*, it wouldn't work for your character's background. Bonnie and Clyde didn't speak with Italian vowels, so why warm up the cast with them?

I'm sure I'll get pushback from this, but it does seem like I'm being the only graduate from The Royal School of the Bleedin' Obvious. Why not embed the job you're going to be doing that night and use the music and the *vowel shapes* of the characters or the geographical setting? Isn't that more appropriate, more helpful, more professional?

In short, do not divorce your warmup from the task ahead – include the genre you're about to sing, embrace it, build from it, create little sequences from it. After all, you don't find athletes on the track 5 minutes before a sprint race warming up by playing rugby. Use your warmup *from the start* to prepare you for the specific task ahead.

Cheers,

Jeremy

PS. When is a classical scale/arpeggio sequence right for a warmup? When you're singing music with classical scales and arpeggios in it. Then it's perfect.

PPS. We talk in detail about what a warmup is and does, three different types of warmup, and six different areas of your voice that need warming up, in our bestselling online training Webinar "What's In A Warmup".

* * *

# TEA BREAK

It must be 4 o'clock. Time for tea. Remember to make the water *really hot.* Mine is Ceylon, weak, black with 1 sugar. And while the kettle is boiling, try your hand at this, the musical theatre quiz to end all musical theatre quizzes. It's multiple choice so choose wisely – you could be a West End Wizard or just West End Woeful.

# THE "MAYBE THIS TIME I'LL BE LUCKY" MUSICALS QUIZ

Love musicals? Think you know all the lyrics? Here are 40 song lyrics from musicals. Some are easy, some just a little trickier, but don't panic, this is a multiple-choice quiz! Choose the line you think finishes the lyric the best.

1. **On my own, pretending**
    a. To be an aeroplane
    b. Takeaway pizza is healthy
    c. He's beside me
2. **He's here, the…**
    a. Plumber
    b. Loser you're dating
    c. Phantom of the Opera
3. **Hello young lovers…**
    a. Whoever you are
    b. That's quite a selfie
    c. Can you stop doing that on the bus?
4. **Feed the birds…**
    a. Until they explode
    b. To the cat
    c. Tuppence a bag
5. **There's a bright golden haze on…**
    a. My porridge
    b. Three-mile island
    c. The meadow
6. **Hello Dolly, it's so nice to…**
    a. Find a sheep that understands
    b. See you back where you belong
    c. Hang upside down smeared in honey but how's your day been?
7. **Defying…**
    a. Logic
    b. Gravity
    c. Everyone because NOBODY UNDERSTANDS ME

8. **Whatever happened to…**
    a. My Facebook account
    b. My hairline
    c. Class
9. **That funny…**
    a. Honey of mine
    b. Noise when I sit down
    c. Sore bit
10. **Dance ten, looks…**
    a. Meh
    b. Constipated
    c. Three
11. **I dreamed a dream in…**
    a. Kinky boots
    b. Time gone by
    c. Stead of paying attention in class
12. **All I want is…**
    a. A room somewhere
    b. To be on *The Only Way Is Essex*
    c. Apparently not available on the NHS
13. **Everything's coming up…**
    a. And it's most inconvenient
    b. Roses
    c. I shouldn't have had kippers and custard for breakfast
14. **When you got it…**
    a. Put some cream on it
    b. Flaunt it
    c. Don't give it to me
15. **What good is sitting alone in your room…**
    a. Come to the cabaret
    b. Come and babysit while I go to the cabaret
    c. You could at least clean it once in a while
16. **The hills are alive…**
    a. With the sound of mucus
    b. With the sound of music
    c. And they're waiting to pounce

**17. Me and my girl, made…**
  a. Out
  b. In Taiwan
  c. For each other

**18. Whenever I feel afraid, I…**
  a. Attack
  b. Hold my head erect
  c. Imagine the audition panel naked

**19. Shall we dance…**
  a. On a bright cloud of music
  b. Or shall I just take your order madam?
  c. No

**20. They say that falling in love is…**
  a. Wonderful
  b. Messy
  c. Lucrative

**21. I hate…**
  a. Men
  b. All men
  c. You (you're a man)

**22. I can show you…**
  a. Around
  b. The world
  c. The next line has been blocked by the British Board of Film Classification

**23. High on a hill stood a lonely goatherd…**
  a. The dating agency really wasn't getting it right
  b. Lay ee odl lay ee odl lay hee hoo
  c. Then he used Clean-A-Baa soap with patented Goat-Remove formula™ for just $29 dollars and he ain't lonely no more!

**24. They live in…**
  a. Hope
  b. You
  c. Essex

**25. I've never been in…**
  a. Love before
  b. Lace before
  c. Pottermore

26. **I got my fingers, got my legs, I got my feet, got my toes, I got my liver, got my blood, I got my guts, I got my muscles, I got…**
    a. My anatomy exam tomorrow
    b. To go to the bathroom
    c. LIFE
27. **I don't know how to…**
    a. Change a lightbulb
    b. Stay in tune
    c. Love him
28. **Tell me it's not…**
    a. You
    b. The dog again
    c. True
29. **My funny**
    a. Little way of doing things
    b. Valentine
    c. Rash
30. **One…**
    a. Singular sensation
    b. Singular tautological numeric reference
    c. Pint of lager and a packet of crisps please
31. **Ten minutes ago…**
    a. I uploaded a photo and it's already gone viral
    b. I saw you
    c. I had a fully charged iPhone
32. **In your Easter bonnet with all the frills upon it…**
    a. You'll be the grandest lady at the Easter parade
    b. Are you sure that yellow goes with the chartreuse?
    c. You look ridiculous Geoff
33. **I remember…**
    a. I came into this room for something
    b. Trees
    c. Getting a show, a meal & a cab for a fiver, but you tell the youth of today that and they won't believe you

**34. Matchmaker, matchmaker…**

a. Make me a match, find me a find, catch me a catch
b. Make me a match, although obviously I'd prefer a man
c. Make me a match, I'm a twisted Firestarter

**35. Jamie is…**

a. Over and Jamie is gone
b. In the kitchen with the turkey twizzlers
c. Gonna choose someone else to be with – No you are, yes Jamie that's exactly what you're doing

**36. Well well well well well well well well well well…**

a. We meet again Mr Bond
b. Will wonders never cease
c. That's ten shale gas wells in that field alone

**37. I got the sun in the morning…**

a. And I moon at night
b. And the moon at night
c. And I was sick for a week

**38. Do you hear the people sing…**

a. Can we get some autotune on that?
b. Singing the song of angry men
c. Just bang on the wall, they'll shut up eventually

**39. Midnight, not a..**

a. Sign of the pizza
b. Sound from the pavement
c. Great time to sunbathe

**40. It's just a jump to the left…**

a. And then a step to the right
b. No, that's your left, not my left
c. Look, it's just a jump ok? Are you sure you should be auditioning for *Cats*?

* * *

# MORE TOP VOCAL TECHNIQUES AND TIPS

## PANT, WOBBLE AND CRY: EXERCISES FOR SINGING WITH VIBRATO

I have had several actors arrive in my studio with the question "how can I learn to sing vibrato?" They complain that their singing is straight and are searching for the warmth and roundness that they hear other singers producing.

Singing with vibrato depends on the repertoire you sing, the emotion you want to portray, and the genre in which you perform. It also depends on personal and societal taste – I am occasionally surprised at the extremes of vibrato that appear in performances of both 19th-century opera and 21st-century musical theatre. Still, one man's bleat is another man's shimmer.

**Here are four areas to explore when searching for "your vibrato"**

1. **Breath fluctuation** – think The Bee Gees or Cliff Richard, also singing actors such as Michael Ball. The breath flow, usually constant when holding a note, is altered to produce a fluctuation. This produces an apparent change in pitch at vocal fold level, caused by under-and over-feeding of air to the vocal folds. This is usually done by using either the abdominal muscles or the ribs in tiny "in-and-out" movements. If you like this sound, you can access it using an exaggerated panting, and then fine it down. As with all vibrato methods, make sure you can switch this one off at will, otherwise sustained singing might become a problem.

2. **Good old pitch changing** – the actual pitch of the note (the speed at which your vocal folds vibrate) is changed, rapidly and smoothly. One exercise for accessing this is to sing a slow semitone trill (oscillate between two notes a semitone apart) and gently speed up, blurring the two notes together. Whether you trill to the semitone below or the semitone above is a matter of personal taste.

3. **Back off! –** another key to this one is relaxation – hold a pitch and then relax your vocal mechanism and "back off" the sound slightly. This tends to bring in an easy gentle oscillation that is quite subtle. As with all vibrato methods, make sure you can switch this one on and off at will, otherwise moving between notes in certain styles might become a problem.

4. **Have a good moan** – sometimes referred to as "cry" or "whine" position. This is "vibrato from the inside" if you like, and is usually quite subtle, more of a warming of the sound. To access this, use your speaking voice to make a whining or moaning sound, then hold the sound/position and sing a note.

Be sure to use only a small amount of breath (holding the breath back a little seems to help in accessing this vocal set). Gillyanne's book *Singing and the Actor* has a good description of this. As with all vibrato methods, make sure you can switch this one off at will, otherwise fast singing (words or notes) might become a problem.

In order to give a rounded picture, I am adding a fifth possibility, although I think it has very specific uses: shaking the instrument itself. This comes in two forms – larynx movement and jaw/tongue shake.

Larynx movement is used by some opera and gospel singers, particularly at high volumes. The larynx can move up and down "freely" on a single note. While there can be a feeling of "letting go" with this style, when taken to extreme it is sometimes difficult to identify which note is being sung as the entire mechanism shudders in the gale. I witnessed a solo singer in a Las Vegas show who allowed her larynx to fluctuate slowly in a vibrato covering a horrifying major 6th.

Jaw/tongue shake uses a similar device – the back of the tongue or the lower jaw (or both) move up and down, causing the sound to oscillate. This version can become addictive so make sure you can switch it off. However, jaw shake (and even head shake) is now being used in contemporary commercial singing as a device for adding tiny vibrato-like trills, particularly in R&B. Use it sparingly.

In my experience, most singers use a combination of 2 and 3, or 3 and 4, depending on the music, the emotion and the context, so I encourage you to experiment with all the versions.

We live in a world of comparison, so I often encourage my clients to do it "wrong". Sometimes you can only discover what you want to do by deliberately not doing it. Experiment with exaggerating each version, then the following fixes for excessive use.

1. **For excessive breath fluctuation** – one of the fixes for this is to practise the sustained hiss, re-educating the muscles of expiration to work smoothly.

2. **For excessive laryngeal movement** – one of the fixes is to use the external anchoring muscles (back of the neck, possibly

the soft palate), and to reduce the airflow slightly, rebalancing the combination of breath, sound and body.

3. **For excessive moaning** – one of the fixes is to use voiced fricatives (vv, zz, zh) to "unhook" and return to a neutral laryngeal position. We also recommend using a "boring" voice, taking out any hint of emotion, to reset the laryngeal position.

And finally, over to Louis Moreau Gottschalk, American pianist-virtuoso, who wrote in 1900:

> *"Tremolo of the voice is the result of either of the three following causes – diseased vocal organs, old age, or defective breathing, and as such has no excuse for its existence."*

You have been warned…

* * *

## FRONT FOOT, BACK FOOT – CHANGING YOUR VOCAL ENERGY

There are many ways to shape musical or dramatic phrases – with dynamics, with tempo, with rhythmic intensity or variation.

Here is an exercise that will work in any musical genre and is also effective for speeches in the theatre and the wedding reception. I use it with high-energy performers to help them grade their performances. For this exercise you will need a favourite song, speech or phrase.

First, let's prepare for the front/back exercise. Stand up with one foot slightly in front of the other, about shoulder width apart. Your weight should be evenly distributed between both feet to begin with. Stand on the outside of your feet, so that your weight is pushing outwards slightly. Now stand on the inside edge of your feet, with your weight pushing inwards slightly. Move your weight to your heels, then move your weight to your toes. Finally, stand with your weight balanced on the centre of both feet, evenly distributed.

You may notice now that you have a habitual stance, on the outside or inside edge, or slightly back or forwards.

Now let's examine the physicality of the front/back foot idea. Move your weight now onto your front foot. You may find yourself leaning forwards, or you may be able to balance successfully without the lean. Nevertheless, more of your weight will be on your front foot, with less on your back foot. This has an inherent emotional and directional feel. The emotional feel is more urgent, faster, more aggressive, more pressing. The directional feel is forwards and either down or up, depending on how your weight is balanced. You might also feel narrower in your upper body, and your breathing might change or feel different. Now sing your favourite song or start your favourite speech, staying on the front foot. Notice the feeling of your body and emotions as you continue your vocal task, staying on your front foot.

Now do the opposite. Move your weight onto your back foot. You may find yourself leaning backwards, or you might be able to shift your weight backwards easily without the lean. Notice the inherent emotion and directional feel. This feels less urgent, more "laid back", slower, even more accepting. The directional feel is backwards and either up or down, depending on how you are balanced.

You might also feel wider and more open in your body, and your breathing might alter. Sing your favourite song or start your best speech again, staying on the back foot. Notice how your body feels, and what emotions emerge as you continue to speak or sing, staying on your back foot.

Now do the same song or speech, but this time stay balanced upright with your weight equally on both feet. Notice the emotions and the feelings in your body that arise.

These different "directions" are used constantly in music or drama – many pieces have phrases or sentiments that have a forward, urgent feel and others that have a more laid-back, lazier feel. This form of tension and release in the phrasing is something that experienced performers can use consciously. Many comedians and presenters use the front foot/back foot technique to encourage an audience to laugh, applaud or quieten.

It's a simple and effective way to add interest and variation to your performing.

You can watch me teaching Front Foot Back Foot to an audience of singers and singing teachers in our streaming video Mastering Musical Theatre, hosted by our colleague Oren Boder on OB1.co.uk

* * *

## LEARNING AND MEMORIZING LYRICS AND LINES

Many performers have mixed feelings towards the business of learning and memorizing. Some see it as a necessary evil, some as a pathway to freedom of expression, some as a visceral connection with their material. Different people use different modes of learning to take in and understand what happens around them and to process information. If you are a teacher, an awareness of these is useful as matching modes with your student will help their understanding and your patience! Neuro Linguistic Programming (NLP) was originally devised to study and reproduce patterns of excellence, and has identified several different modes of learning, including visual, auditory and kinaesthetic.

Learning and memorizing are different processes, and it is important to separate the two. It can be time-consuming to correct something that has been learned imperfectly, so the first task is to learn the music accurately. Take a little time to check every note, every rhythm and every word. This does not necessarily mean that you must spend hours poring over the score, merely to be aware of each note and rhythm as you read it. Singers have the added difficulty of dealing with words and storyline. Following the notes and words with a pencil or finger while singing seems to focus the attention and can help highlight tiny problem areas.

### *Learn a Song in 15 Minutes*

I have found that the following 5-step learning process is the most effective and fastest way to ensure accuracy. This process appears in more detail in the Conscious Learning chapter of the book *Successful Singing Auditions*, co-written with Gillyanne Kayes.

**Step One**
Read the words of your chosen song as a script or conversation to connect with the story.

**Step Two**
Speak the words in the written rhythm. Make sure to elongate any syllables on long notes, holding them for the full amount. Notice where the diphthongs or vowel changes occur, and if any words now have different stresses. Look out for unusual sounds and places to breathe.

**Step Three**
Listen once to the melody, then siren through it (sing very quietly on *ng*). Slide gently between the notes for maximum effect and to teach the intervals to your vocal muscles.

**Step Four**
Miren the song. Mirening means mouthing the words at the front of the mouth while maintaining the *ng* hum at the back. Make sure to form all the consonants that are made near the front of the mouth – l, m, f, etc. Use the same size lip and jaw movements as if you were speaking – you do not need to exaggerate.

**Step Five**
Sing the words and melody together.

### *Memorizing a Song*

Learning music can be a whole-brain experience, and all the tools listed below have worked with my singing students, singly or in combination.

- **Intellectual**: using word links, alliteration and assonance, onomatopoeia, meaning, verbal and intellectual understanding, pitching and rhythm
- **Non-intellectual**: finding shape, texture, feel, emotion, movement, direction, colour, imagery, melody shape and rhythmic impetus
- **Physical**: hand shapes and gestures, drawing shapes in the air, and identifying "oddities" such as accidentals in phrases, unexpected or awkward intervals, unusual movements in the music or words

- **Sensing**: internal = muscle memory, pitch/feel awareness, emotional links; external = physical positioning on stage and movement of body / plotting the song / other characters.

### *Moving From Assimilation to Recall*

Some singers find learning the music and text together the most efficient way of memorizing. For some it is simply a case of repetition and more repetition until it "goes in". One of my clients memorizes in the bath as the relaxed atmosphere and flattering acoustic help her retain information. Comfortable as this may sound, what are the strategies when relearning something that has been learned incorrectly? I have worked with Hatstand Opera as a musical director and coach for several years, and the company's opera singers use a different approach to memorizing and correcting.

### *What Type of Learner Are You?*

#### Auditory

Tenor Richard needs to hear me sing the phrase in the inaccurate version that he has just made, followed by the accurate version so that he can compare the sounds. Auditory clients can use the following techniques: hearing internally before you sing, being aware of other characters (real or imaginary) moving or speaking around you, onomatopoeia, mimicry, recording yourself singing the piece to help memory and save voice, using accompaniments to learn the harmonic structure, and listening for "where the sound fits".

#### Visual

Soprano Toni needs to see the music and words at same time. When dealing with a problem phrase, explanation or demonstration does not work as she needs to see the written page "to get the whole pattern and where it goes – even though I'm not a great sightreader Iknow the shape and can see where it fits". Those with a visually biased memory can use the following techniques: visualizing the shape of phrase, noting the page layout, turning the story/words into imagery as a detailed photograph or TV film sequence, using colours to express the emotions, drawing or pictures of the piece (visual kinaesthetic).

## Kinaesthetic

Mezzo Kirsty understands feel and emotion language and will work best when given the emotional temperature or dramatic purpose for a correction. When memorizing music Kirsty paces the kitchen, as moving helps her to integrate the music and words. Several times in performance she "does not know what's coming next" but has trusted her muscle memory enough to open her mouth and allow her muscles to take over, producing the correct words at the appropriate time. Kinaesthetic clients can use the following tools: write or type the words, feel the curves of the phrases, identifying and untangling the knots in memory. It is important with kinaesthetic clients to allow them to move. Any amount of movement will suffice, from slight shifting of weight to bouncing off the walls. Bodily movements, even if apparently unconnected, will help these clients to integrate voice, memory and understanding.

## Changing language

Many of my singing clients consider themselves "primarily" dancers, actors or instrumentalists. In my own case, piano playing is my most established form of musical physicality (I've been performing for more than 30 years). Translating instructions into the language familiar to the client can often increase the speed and depth of understanding. As a pianist I often use my hands to add "fingering" to the singing phrases – moving my fingers, even microscopically by my side, can help me retain difficult vocal intervals and phrase patterns. Violin phrasing, oboe articulation and dance positions have all had their place in my coaching sessions.

## Using recordings

Commercially available recordings are useful for discovering new repertoire or identifying stylistic nuances. I encourage my clients to listen once for an overview of the piece: the shape and emotion, orchestration and temperature, the general tessitura. However, I discourage listening for performance tips from another singer, as each singer's instrument is different, and their style may be personal or even dated.

Record your own version using the music – you hear your own voice and nuances, and you can be confident that the singing is musically accurate. If you are unsure of your musical ability it is best to ask a pianist experienced in your repertoire to record your song for you. I tend to record at least two different versions for my singing clients, the melody at a slower pace with simple chordal accompaniment, and the full accompaniment without the vocal line played at the appropriate speed. There is nothing wrong with working at "thinking speed", a quarter to a half slower than normal. I also encourage my clients to record their sessions.

**Getting help**

Many singers find memorizing easier with outside help combining intellectual and emotional responses – using a coach to reflect, enhance, and question can help clarify original decisions and provides a sounding board for discussion and input. It is a simple matter to focus on an "accuracy run", with the coach acting as another pair of ears to highlight any corners that have escaped you. A speed run can be an exhilarating way of discovering how well you know a piece. Many singers find having a coaching session acts as a deadline, an impetus to memorize.

Learning music is about understanding the printed page. Memorizing is about owning the piece, taking it into your body and psyche, and expressing your self through that composer's language, discovering the concepts that lie behind the notes. Memorizing takes performance to another level as "getting it accurate" becomes "bringing it to life".

*This article first appeared in the Music Teacher magazine and appears by kind permission of Rhinegold Publishing.*

* * *

## RHYTHM AND PULSE FOR COOL, SWINGING SINGING

You don't have to sing louder or higher to make the music swing – it's all in the beat. Here's a story of a coaching session I gave in Stockholm recently where I used the Rhythm and Pulse exercise to help a singer give a much cooler, stronger performance.

During a musical theatre class, one singer arrived with the piece "What's the Buzz" from *Jesus Christ Superstar*, the Andrew Lloyd

Webber and Tim Rice musical. He was performing it well, but his whole body was involved with the (very fast) pulse inherent in the song. He was bouncing with every eighth note and was displaying a highly tensioned body that was detracting from his performance, both vocally and as an actor.

In the song, the ensemble sings "What's the buzz, tell me what's a happenin'" repeatedly, with high energy. His character then must interrupt them, stop them chattering and calm them down in a very short space of time. He starts with three quarter notes (crotchets) beginning on a high F, which should silence them immediately. Because he was using the same frenetic pulse as the ensemble, his entry was having little impact, and the feel of his performance was not strong enough. Rather than getting him to sing stronger or higher, I took him through the following exercise for finding a different pulse.

1. This involves using your body, so standing is best. Sing the first few phrases of an up-tempo song, such as "What's the Buzz". Find the fast energy of the piece and move to it, using your foot, leg, body or clicking your fingers. "What's the Buzz" has four quarter notes to each bar, but for this exercise I'd like you to move on the eighth notes (quavers). So, for example, your foot taps on the beat and your fingers click on the offbeat. The important thing is to have some part of your body moving on every eighth note.

2. Now we're going to change the pulse while keeping the "speed" the same. Begin to indicate only the quarter notes – you are now moving in "half time". Keep the energy high but move only on the quarter notes. Again, you can either move your body to each quarter note, or divide the quarter notes between foot and hand. The speed of the piece stays the same, but the pulse has now changed to a less frantic one.

3. Now begin to indicate only the half notes (minims). Again, keep the speed of the piece the same, and keep the energy high. Now you are only marking two pulses per measure instead of the four or eight previously. The speed of the piece has stayed the same, but the feel is now different, with a bigger scope, somehow funkier.

You can continue with this exercise, using one pulse per measure, or even one pulse per two measures.

In the case of the singer in the masterclass, the use of a different pulse was electrifying. By using a different, slower pulse (the halfnote or minim rhythm) against the rhythm of the chorus around him (eighth note or quaver rhythm) he was able to differentiate himself from them, and stop their beat in its tracks. This easily marked out his character (Jesus) as a man to be listened to, who did not march to the beat of the people around him. By following this exercise, the singer was able to convey that effortlessly.

I have used this exercise in many different genres of music, including opera arias ("O zittre nicht", "Questa o quella"), German lieder ("Gretchen am Spinnrade"), music by contemporary commercial music singers such as Duffy or Christina Aguilera, and of course musical theatre pieces from *West Side Story* to *Spring Awakening*. Try it for yourself!

* * *

## LOSE THE DEAD FISH LOOK, OR HOW TO SING THE SONG INTRO

You sing well, you make great sounds and you can put a song across.

Why do you look like a dead fish in the song intro?

Most singers identify with melody, shape or lyrics, and many come alive when they are communicating through them. But the song intro and postlude are part of the song experience for the audience. Of course, the singer doesn't sing during them.

It's one of my pet hates in auditions: the pianist has started the song, but the singer just isn't present, and by the beginning of the postlude the singer has already gone for a coffee. It demonstrates two things – no respect for the pianist, and no understanding of the song's purpose, its atmosphere and when it begins and ends.

Here's an exercise to help singers deal with the wordless parts of a song intro:

1. The first question to ask is: when does the song start? You might SAY when the first note of the intro starts (or even before) but do you DO it? Ask the pianist to play (or listen to a performance track of) only the song intro and the interludes (the gaps where you don't sing). What emotions does each unsung piece of music create? Is it what you expect or does it undercut the first line of the lyrics? You might like to add some words or descriptive phrases, or just give yourself a colour, a mood or a shape to focus on before you sing.

2. In the Vocal Process Webinar on Exams, Auditions and Competitions we introduced the "Answers on a Postcard" technique to help you find your way immediately into the song. Use it here to identify the mood, emotion and feel of the intro.

3. Think of your eyeline. Do you want to make eye contact with the audience at all? If so, when? When the pianist starts the song intro, when you start singing, or later on a meaningful phrase?

4. If you don't want to eyeball the audience (if it's not in the character's best interests), decide whether you're going to use your chosen focus point before you sing or when you sing. If the latter, where are you going to focus as a pre-singing point? And why?

5. Making the introduction (and the interludes) work without speaking or singing forces you to think through what happens to the character when they don't sing. It also helps you understand AND memorize song entries and structure.

6. Find the thought at the beginning of the song intro and hold the thought (and your energy and focus) until after all the music has ended. It really helps you *and* your audience process the emotions of the song and lets them get the maximum out of your performance.

And that's pretty useful!

* * *

# PATTER SONGS AND GOOD DICTION

I've always been a fan of patter songs – the type with speedy text or long lists of items. Think "Modern Major General" (Gilbert & Sullivan), or one of the most difficult written for a woman – "Not Getting Married Today" (Sondheim). I've sung them and I've coached them for years.

The thing you don't do when singing patter songs is to produce machine-gun diction, strong volume, or big jaw and lip movements. These are all things that the novice singer thinks will get the words across, but in reality, they make the song less intelligible.

Isn't good diction at speed all about getting every consonant and syllable clear and projected? And shouldn't you have to work your articulators extra hard so that the audience hears every part of every word?

Nope.

## *Everything Depends on Execution*

This is the difference between good diction and good intelligibility. To get the stories and images in patter songs across to the listener, you must be understandable. And if the human ear hears machine-gun consonants delivered at the same level of importance throughout, the human brain gets mesmerized and doesn't "translate" the sounds into words. If you've ever watched the UK TV show *Miranda*, you'll see Miranda getting mesmerized by a word to the point where the word doesn't make sense anymore.

The art of the patter song is to choose certain syllables and de-emphasize the rest. Once you accept that, it's just a case of working out which are the essential syllables and which ones you can throw away.

## *It's Time to Get to Work*

Here's an example. Recently I gave an online coaching session to a soprano on the song "I Love the Way" from the show *Something Rotten*. It's a duet, but we've created a solo version. There are four high-speed lines of text in the song (quavers in a speedy 3/4), so we broke down the rhythm and the critical words.

Bear in mind that the following technique isn't "This Is How This Line Must Go" – I always apply the technique to each singer individually and often we choose a different pattern depending on the singer's voice, energy and the shape and control of their personal articulators (tongue, jaw, lips and soft palate).

Figure 2: Excerpt from "I Love the Way" from *Something Rotten.*

## *Link by Link*

The first line is straightforward: "Every time I hear a perfect rhyme I get all tingly". The important syllables are on the first beat of each bar – Ev and Per – and you can get rid of the rest. And rather than singing the rhythm with robotic accuracy, hold those two important syllables a little longer and rush slightly through the rest.

However, that "on the beat" pattern doesn't work for the second line: "That to find a perfect rhyme is not an easy thingly". Usually, you'd go for That and Rhyme since they're on the first beat of each bar, but you end up tripping over the other words. Using Per and Not gives you a better flow, even though those syllables are on rhythmically weak beats. (Your other option is to use Find and Not which are both on beat 2 in the bar). The first time you'll find this tricky, but your audience will understand the whole sentence much more easily, and you don't have to work as hard.

## *Piece by Piece*

The third line is different again: "(I) love a lilting line of lyrical alliteration". The main beats are Love and Lyr, but the tricky bit is getting your tongue around all the back-and-forward consonants (l, t, ng, l, n, l, c, l, etc). This needs a 2-part solution.

First, practise saying the six syllables "lyrical alliter…" without moving your lips or jaw in any way. Let the tongue itself do all the work. This is a ventriloquial exercise, and it's why I recommend all patter song singers read the ventriloquism chapter in our book *This Is A Voice.* It contains many useful exercises for separating the movements of tongue, jaw and lips!

Second, sing the whole line and put a slight emphasis (and a hold) on the syllables Lil and Lyr (beat 2 and beat 1 respectively).

### ***Putting It Together***

Once you've put those two solutions together, the line just trips off the tongue.

The fourth line is "when the phrases come together like a consummation". The main beats are When and Geth, but it helps both the intelligibility and the comedy if you emphasize and linger slightly on the Come and Con.

### ***Adding Up to Make a Work of Art***

This entire coaching sequence with my soprano took just 7 minutes, and by the end she was very comfortable singing the song. It's now gone into her portfolio for other auditions.

*PS If you're wondering where the headings come from, it's Sondheim's "Putting It Together" from Sunday In The Park With George*

* * *

## COACHING SINGING IN FRENCH

Well, that was an interesting day.

Today I found myself unexpectedly coaching in French with an emergency singer. Sorry, that came out wrong – he is a singer wanting a coaching session immediately, not a singer who only bursts into song during crises…

### ***Standard Problems Singing in French (or German)***

He was singing a contemporary rock musical translated into French and was having trouble with some of the sounds required. I find it fascinating working with people in different languages. It's surprising how many singing problems are caused by vowels that don't work for that particular singer/voice, or consonants that aren't in the right place or are worked too hard. Many singers don't understand the difference between voiced and unvoiced consonants, and while most voiced consonants can be pitched, some are difficult to pitch easily (b, d, g, I'm looking at you).

A few months ago, Gillyanne and I coached an entire cast for *Annie The Musical* in German. We used our knowledge of languages and phonetics, together with our expertise in vocal function, to help the singers make the sung language work. Any language has voiced and unvoiced consonants, but if you're singing in a language that isn't your mother tongue, or you're singing a translation from the original, you may be bringing over your habitual consonant use in a way that isn't appropriate for the new version.

### *Singing Consonants on High Notes*

For my client today, most of the translation into French works well but there are, as always, some awkward or unusual words on high notes. I did study French A Level about 95 years ago, and so I had an idea of the shapes and consonant usage – but I'm an extremely rusty speaker (meaning I lack practice, rather than having random orange bits drop off me…). I'm relying on my client to pronounce the words accurately. Much of the writing for his character's songs sits around E4–G4, a slightly tricky area for a baritone to stay in. He sings very good clear French, but because of the height of the pitches in certain phrases, there's one sound we need to modify.

The word *tout* ("all") appears on several Es and Fs, and his classic pronunciation had so much lip rounding and such a narrow vowel shape inside that there was almost no sound coming out. And of course, it felt incredibly tight to sing and disturbed his vocal line. We worked to keep the essence of the "ou" vowel but with a vowel closer to a schwa inside the mouth and keeping the extended lip pout but with a slightly bigger opening between the lips.

We still have enough "ou" in the vowel for listeners to understand it (and to stop them thinking his pronunciation was bad) but the different resonating space and wider exit made the passaggio notes much easier to sing and sustain.

Client is happy, and I get to work in a different language.

Cheers (À votre santé!)

If you want to find out more about potential problems and fixes for singing words, check out our online masterclass here Mastering Musical Theatre.

* * *

## BELTING THE MONEY NOTE

I'm at the studios in London's West End for my regular coaching sessions.

Today seems to be troubleshooting day, and I thought I'd share one noteworthy session.

My client was having problems with belting the money note in a song (the song title escapes me at the moment – must be middle age creeping in).

The second half of the song sits up around F and G, and the final note is a long held G on the word "go". since he has easy high A's, he couldn't work out why the G was so taxing. I broke down the task into its separate components.

### *The Word Components*

The g of "go" didn't seem to be causing problems, but the vowels were. He was trying to close down onto the second vowel of the diphthong (like the conscientious singer he is). We experimented with different vowels for the diphthong – Ah Oh (or the vowels in "cart hot") worked best in this case, but you may need to experiment yourself for a better personal choice. Some vowels may need to be modified in belting to get the sound you want without losing too much of the word.

Doing "Gah-oh" worked superbly for him – giving him an open and exciting belt sound, a clearer first vowel, and helping him avoid closing down too much for the second vowel. This change pretty much solved the problem, so there were only two tweaks left.

### *The Note*

The G isn't really in his belt range, it's just underneath, so vocally it feels a little odd. Even though he wasn't in a vocal belt setup, by putting him in a physical belt position (body braced, head up "to the gods", the sound got just a little thicker and easier without him weighting his voice anymore. It also looks good!

### *The Ending*

Coming off a belt note can be tricky if you're not completely balanced. We explored different tone offsets, including glottal offset (which sounds like a truck into a brick wall, frankly, but could be useful for shock value), and chose the slight pitch bend downwards for best effect. So, his pattern was hit the note in "belt position", hold it absolutely straight until the last few seconds, add the vibrato, and drop the pitch around a tone just as he offset the sound.

Working well so far…

### *Applause!*

And for more applause we added a delay to the word of a couple of beats, and a gasp offset right at the end. Shockingly corny I know, but it builds the intensity of the performance without having to do it vocally. And in this song, corny works.
Client was pleased that the fix was so straightforward (and quick).

Well, that's 25 years of experience, and that's what you pay me for.

***Update. Client just emailed to remind me that the song is "She Was There" from *The Scarlet Pimpernel.* End of senior moment***

*   *   *

The next section focuses on changing genre. What do you have to do to move from one style of music to another – which techniques and style features can you keep and which do you need to change to sound authentic? Read on…

# CROSSING GENRES – TECHNIQUES TO SING IN A DIFFERENT STYLE

## STYLE CONSCIOUS

The actress Minnie Driver had some interesting comments on her ability to take on an accent or dialect.

Ms Driver is famous for being able to switch accents or assume a dialect successfully and believes that her singing background has helped:

> It's a trick. It's music. I play music a lot. I play a couple of instruments. I think accents come from the same part of your brain. A lot of this is about commitment, you just commit to it, and you pay attention.

I believe those comments about commitment apply to changing both your singing sound quality and the genre/style you sing in. When you first decide to change your singing sound quality or expand your palette of vocal colours (having not done it before), each new colour sounds and feels odd. You work with a coach to embed the new information, and to make sure that your version is accurate and healthy, and then you start to commit to it, to make it sound and feel your own.

The same applies to changing musical style. First comes the inclination to change, usually from having heard something that you would like to be able to do. Then you find (or are shown) the techniques to be able to make those changes. And finally you commit to making those musical decisions, to believing yourself in that musical genre. And you pay attention while you are doing it until it becomes "second nature".

Here is a collection of articles on changing vocal and music style, starting with moving from classical to contemporary.

For the purposes of this article I will assume that you are a singer with classical-based training, wishing to change your singing style to sing (in English) in a more contemporary style.

Let's look first at one of the most misunderstood concepts in classical singing:

## 1. VOCAL LINE OR MUSICAL PHRASING

Cutting or interrupting the line is probably the biggest single thing you can alter to change your singing style.

A standard classical phrase usually arches up from the first note and arches down to the last note. The ideal is uninterrupted sound, evenly matched throughout. In more contemporary styles, matching the sound throughout is less important, as words and specific emotions take centre stage. There is usually no inbuilt need to sustain projected tone over a large orchestra, so delivery is more colloquial. Actors compare this to the difference in delivery between stage and screen acting.

Take the first few lines of a song and speak them as if on the phone to a close friend. Notice where you breathe (many people take breaths in the middle of sentences) and which words you emphasize. The important thing here is to be intimate.

You can cut the vocal line whenever you like, if you have a good dramatic reason for doing so. This often goes completely against classical training, so I use the following simple exercise to introduce breaking the line.

***An Exercise for Breaking Out of the Classical Phrasing Style***

i. Choose a phrase and speak it several times, breathing after a different word each time.

ii. If you are successful on the first attempt, you can add the idea that each breath point must make sense dramatically. My clients are usually surprised at the number of dramatic reasons you can find doing this exercise – chasing a thought, panicked in-breath, awe, lost for words, pause for emphasis.

iii. Repeat the exercise using the break but without breathing.

iv. Now sing the same phrase using the gaps, hesitations or cutting short of words that you have discovered in the spoken version.

v. The results include a more authentic use of text, a change of focus from sound to meaning, and a freedom in performance. If you are running out of breath in a performance, you can cut the line and alter the shape of the phrase without losing the dramatic intensity.

And it's not cheating!

## 2. BREATH AND YOUR SINGING STYLE

A highly contentious subject; almost everyone has thoughts about breath, whether it's what they should be doing or can't do, or whether they don't have enough (very rarely do they think they have too much).

I wish to lay my cards on the table – **one size does not fit all**. Different phrases require different amounts of breath, as do different voice qualities, different vocal styles and different tessituras. There is not even one breathing pattern or habit that can successfully sustain all the different vocal styles.

The most important points of breathing are:

- how much air do you take in?
- where do you take it in?
- do you need to store it?
- how much do you let out?
- how do you control it?

Many budding crossover singers are locked into a single breathing pattern, taking in a specified amount of air and holding it back until the end of the phrase (however long). You may have already discovered from cutting the line that breathing patterns in contemporary music are much more flexible. How do you notice your own breathing patterns?

***An Exercise to Identify Your Breathing Patterns***

Take a musical phrase and sing it through in one breath. Then take in half your normal amount of air and sing it again. Then take in a quarter of your normal amount of air and sing it again. What do you notice? Can you feel yourself going into negative pressure? Where you are squeezing to find the air?

Now take in a much larger amount of air than normal and sing the phrase again. What do you notice at the beginning? At the end? This exercise helps my clients find the optimum amount of air for the phrase out of context.

***An Exercise Using Different Breath Patterns***

Take the same musical phrase and use the "cutting the line" exercises to discover different shapes in the phrase. Each different shape will require a different amount of air, because you have numerous opportunities to top up. The same phrase can require different amounts of air depending on its meaning, volume and setting.

## 3. WORD DECAY

Decay focuses on the shaping of individual words, particularly on long notes. The emphasis in classical generic terms is on a full sustaining of the sound to the end of the note <=====, or occasionally <======>. But when you change your singing style, decay can be used as an expressive tool and usually becomes more exaggerated as the music becomes more contemporary.

There are various shapes you can follow, including long sustain with late, medium decay ======>>, or swift increase of volume/tone followed by long decay <===>>>>>>.

More extreme versions can include:

=>----------
or ====>-------
or even =>--------<==.

Experiment with the positioning, the length and the speed of your decay. The use of decay is bolder in contemporary singing style, with adjoining words often having completely different decay patterns. Listen to Frank Sinatra for a stylish and effective combination of word decay.

## 4. VOWELS

Sorry, classical singers, but when changing your singing style, those seven Italian vowels simply will not do. The English language has more than 20 recognized vowel sounds, and contemporary music uses all of them. These include the vowels in "hit", "nurse" and of course, "love" (not lav, lawv or lurve). Singers usually find that some English vowels are more "difficult" to sing than others. This is partly "muscle memory" (they haven't yet built the correct brain pathways) and partly a diction setup issue.

Gillyanne Kayes in her book *Singing and the Actor* introduces the concept of vowel medialization. In brief, matching the vowels to an /i:/ (EE) position makes the more unusual vowels much easier to produce and helps with clearer and more understandable diction. Tone is more forward, and the tongue works less hard for better results. For authenticity, learn to sing ALL the English vowels. And if you want to sing pop, rock and soul music and American musical theatre, explore Standard American and "Motown" vowels.

## 5. DIPHTHONGS

These are useful emotional and textual devices and deserve a subcategory of their own. Diphthongs can be managed in several ways:

- Late and fast: favoured by conscientious classical singers, the first vowel is held to almost the end of the note and the second vowel is popped in at the last moment (so "why" becomes something like "whaaaaaaaaai").

- Early and fast: some CCM singers use this device, much parodied elsewhere ("whyeeeeeee").

- Middle and fast: the diphthong changes in the middle of the note-length and the arrival on the second vowel is swift ("whaaaiiiii").

- Middle and slow: the diphthong changes in the middle of the note-length, but the travel to the second vowel is slow. This can add colour and emotion to a long note and is a favourite of mine ("whaa-eh-i-ii").

## 6. CONSONANTS

Using consonants with accuracy is the quickest way of getting detailed emotion into your singing style. The way to deal with consonants is to find exactly where the obstruction occurs and to do it there and nowhere else. All consonants require either partial or full obstruction of the vocal tract. Partial obstruction means the air and sound moves through or past a narrowing – such as the first sound in "vie". Full obstructions are caused by a total blocking of the vocal tract – such as the first sound in "pie".

### *An Exercise to Identify Different Consonant Features*

Take a sentence and break it down into vowel and consonant sounds. Then see, hear, feel, taste where the consonant is made and elongate it. This includes holding the stop in a stopped consonant (the completely closed feeling at the beginning of a (t), for example). Beware of trying to exaggerate the consonant by pressing, squeezing or pushing. Stopped consonants (t, d, p, b, k, g) require the airflow and sound to stop momentarily – a problem if your overriding instruction is to keep the line going at all costs. This topic links with both "1. Line" and "2. Breath".

A sub-category is:

### *Consonant Timing*

In classical singing style, consonants are de-emphasized as resonance, projection and matching vowels are prioritized. But bringing in certain consonants early, extending their life and pre-empting or delaying word beginnings and endings can add an enormous amount of audience intelligibility to your singing. In our book *Successful Singing Auditions*, Gillyanne Kayes and I deal extensively with consonant timing.

* * *

## FOCUS YOUR STORY

Singing is not just about making noises, it is about telling a story, portraying a character's life and emotional journey, embodying a situation.

Decide whether your song speaks directly to the audience or whether the audience eavesdrops on the character's life. Bear in mind that this could change depending on the performance situation – I coach performers to move a song from theatre to cabaret to recital room, all of which have different requirements and expectations.

### *Place Your Characters*

Let's assume that you are in character on stage, and the character does not know that the audience exists. Is the song a soliloquy, or a "duet" with someone else (silent) on stage? Are any other people mentioned in the song? It helps to place them or their habitat on stage with you – so the friend you saw yesterday could be placed downstage right and your family (last week) could live stage left. This helps you to focus your thoughts and the audience to understand to whom you are referring. It also helps with continuity if you refer to someone throughout a song. In my work as an audition coach, I will often alter songs for each audition to help the performer find a completely different rendition.

### *Landscaping*

Landscaping involves understanding and changing the shape of the song and the performance, and as such can be applied to a number of song components. Every song has a climax. If you think it has more than one, there is usually one that is bigger than the others. Where does the climax of the song come – the very end, the last page, the middle? Once you have found the climax, sing everything else smaller! This simple rule helps you to plot the entire shape of the performance. If you tend to start too big, or to push your voice during a song, line up your sights on the biggest climax. You will know how to change what you do to accommodate it.

Landscaping applies to phrases, to sections, to whole songs, even to whole roles. Where is the most joyous, painful, emotional or strong moment? Find it and grade everything else below it. Once you have found your peaks, find your valleys and grade them too (they don't have all have to be 1/10).

All these topics will help you change the singing style in which you perform. You may also find that using these exercises helps you to access different vocal qualities more easily. Rejoice in your new flexibility, and above all, enjoy.

*This article first appeared in the Music Teacher magazine and appears by kind permission of Rhinegold Publishing.*

* * *

## MOVING FROM OPERA TO MUSICAL THEATRE STYLE

I'm working in the West End coaching studio again today. I love working with versatile singers, and the opera singer who came today is doing well with more contemporary styles.

In today's 90-minute session we had a Caribbean national anthem, "Jerusalem", "We'll Meet Again", "The Girl in 14G" and a new lyrical musical theatre piece (not heard in this country yet). Normally we'd be doing Donizetti or Mozart, so this is quite a repertoire swing!

This session was about tweaking and guiding. I'm working with her on vocal style, performing tips and watchpoints, and which musical style points belong to which musical genre. It's fascinating for me to hear someone who is so used to singing and working in one genre change to another. She is doing well and has an instinct for communication, although sometimes we have to fight the previous training!

To the lyrical musical theatre piece, we added volume changes within words, breathy excitement to one section, specific diction tips to another and played around with keys until we found one that really worked for her voice. The original was apparently for a female bass - baritone (down to low E and – the highest note – an octave above middle C). She's an operatic soprano singing with a lyrical vocal sound, so we had to find a key that worked with direct communication and didn't "overblow" on the top notes. Apologies to the opera singers reading this article, but I know what I mean! Just ask me if you want to find out more…

We ended up in Eb, a warm key for the song (subtext – "Please don't ask me to leave you, I love you, but I'll never see you again"). Unfortunately, in the middle key change we ended up in Gb major – a great key for warm climaxes, but a little devil to transpose into. Although I prefer people to sing in the original keys most of the time, there are certain styles of music where key is less important than performance, and this style was one of them. It was far more important to get the feel of the music and the emotion across than stick rigidly to the written score, and the transposed key worked far better for her.

Having said that, she'll be working with the composers in a couple of weeks' time, so I expect there's some leeway.

* * *

## COACHING "THE GIRL IN 14G" WITH DIFFERENT SINGERS

"The Girl in 14G" is a great song written to showcase the talents of Kristin Chenoweth. It includes operatic staccato coloratura reminiscent of Mozart's "Queen of the Night", jazz scat, and a mousey narrator who has a personality change. Check out Kristin's recording of it – it's excellent.

It's been fascinating working with different voices on this piece. Mostly they've been trained in musical theatre (usually by Gillyanne Kayes or me), but I also have a working operatic soprano singing it. Since she really does sing "Queen of the Night" professionally, the staccato coloratura sections up to high D hold no terrors for her. Although she does complain that the patterns aren't quite the same and she had to relearn them after 15 years of performing!

I've been working with her on the jazz sound and the sounds for the main character – mousy narrator and Broadway belter. The jazz setup has a low larynx, lowered tongue (with lots of mouth space) and altered vowels, with a breathier voice quality.

The narrator uses what my students refer to as baby twang – small, bright, piercing and definitely not pushed. With this singer we are not using full-on Broadway belt for the finale, but a very good replacement, reinforced twang. It's very effective.

Performing this song contains the added task of moving quickly and safely from one voice quality to another. In my operatic soprano's case she has to "rack down" on the opera sound to match the others. It's endlessly fascinating where singers "live" musically and what strategies I need to give them to adopt and adapt a new style.

* * *

## GETTING HELP WITH LEARNING A NEW STYLE

One idea behind learning a new style is: If you can hear it, you can learn it, and once you have learned it, you can play with it, mould it, modify it, and use it in your own way.

The first thing to do is to separate out the various components of style.

### *Voice Quality*

What is the "default" vocal sound that your singer performs in? Does the basic sound have twang, breath, cry?

- Does the singer use particular vowel sounds or have a particular accent?
- If female, does the singer spend most time in "head" or "chest" voice?
- How does the singer's voice move around – fast riffs (coloratura in classical music), slow sustained phrases, or slow phrases with flurries of notes in?
- How does the singer's voice move between the notes – sliding, clean breaks, jumps?
- Is there vibrato – present all the time, most of the time, only on long notes, not at all?
- How does the singer start and end notes (onset and offset) – glottal, glide, creak, flip, breath push?

As you can see from the list, there are a lot of things to recognize in someone else's performance and to find in your own.

You might be one of the lucky singers who can imitate someone on your first hearing, and get the style, intonation, vocal patterns and riffs right immediately. This is a talent of its own, although it does have drawbacks, including a possible difficulty in finding your own voice and vocal identity. Often it can be difficult to tune your ear into how someone else uses their voice, because they move so fast.

I am going to add to the sentence at the top of the opening paragraph: If you can hear it and **slow it down**, you can learn it accurately.

If you are internet savvy, I have discovered one very useful tool that can help you discover exactly what happens in a fast riff, and what types of vibrato people use. It has a free trial version, and it's called The Amazing SlowDowner. It does exactly what it says in the title. If you load up a sound file (including .wav and mp3), you can play it out through the Amazing SlowDowner at the correct speed or slow it down (without changing the pitch). The programme can slow the recording down enough that you can hear individual notes in a fast run or play it in superslow motion to hear the individual movements in a singer's vibrato. If there is a particularly difficult riff that you need to hear repeatedly, you can play it as a loop, for as long as you need.

Now you can start to tune your ears into the patterns of your chosen singer. You can hear how they start notes – on, above or below the pitch – and what type of onset they use. You can hear whether their vibrato moves underneath, above or around the note (see the section "Pant, Wobble and Cry" for more details). You can hear whether they slide between certain notes or move quickly and cleanly. You can also hear the individual notes of a riff or vocal pattern and learn them more easily.

In answer to a question on singing in different styles, I believe that, once you have discovered what other singers do, you can use the riff patterns and vocal style elements in other songs. You might practise singing a song that your chosen recording artist hasn't recorded but sing it in their style.

This is a very useful exercise as it helps you identify what style elements that artist would use, without copying one performance or song slavishly.

As a performer you can quickly build up a mental and musical catalogue of vocal styles, and use whichever style is most appropriate for that job or that song. The more you work in a style, the more ingrained it becomes, and the more "natural" it sounds.

### *Same Song, Different Vocal Style…*

Recently on one of our intensive vocal training Retreats I thought it was interesting to put in a listening exercise. We played Lea Salonga (creator of the title role in *Miss Saigon* and a musical theatre singer) and Christina Aguilera (pop/R&B diva) singing the same song.

"Reflection" appears in two guises in the same film, *Mulan.* Lea Salonga sings it during the film itself in the character of Mulan. This is a musical theatre performance. Christina Aguilera sings the same number over the end credits, in the style of a pop ballad.

Same song, same key (mostly), same words, different vocal styles, totally different performances.

One person on the Retreat didn't even recognize that it was the same song! In this comparison, it is not just the choice of voice quality that is different – the beginnings and endings of notes and phrases, the emphasis on text and/or emotion, even the melody itself differed between the two performances.

Different approaches really are valid in different genres, and this was a great demonstration that musical and vocal styles are not simply about the sounds you make. In my singing coaching I work not only with different sounds, but also with different approaches to notes, greater or lesser freedom with the written notes, changes of articulation and pronunciation, different onsets and offsets, different architectural structures and different emotional journeys.

I love my job!

* * *

## CHANGING STYLE WITH ONSETS AND OFFSETS

Style is "everything" in the recording industry (actually it isn't, but that's what they'd like us to think…)

So what is *vocal* style?

Style in singing is about the way you use your voice, rather than the actual sound you make. It might be the musical shapes you make with the words and notes (single notes, long phrases, fast flurries of notes on one word). Or even the type of accent or dialect you use when you sing (American, South London "reggae", Motown, "Britpop", operatic, Italian, English, etc).

For this article I'm going to focus on one aspect of vocal style – the way you can start and finish a note. I work with number of singers who are competing in karaoke competitions or working in tribute bands who want to have more choices about the songs they sing or the singers they cover. Here's an exercise I use in my studio to help my singers discover how to change their vocal style.

Each artist usually has a few favourite ways of starting and finishing, so let's explore.

### *Let's Start at the Very Beginning*

Starting a note is called Making the Tone Onset, and it happens right at the beginning of a note, word or phrase.

There are many different ways of onsetting a sound, from the standard three for classical singers to the complex combinations for CCM singers. Let's explore some of the possibilities.

Classical or operatic singers usually use three standard onsets, so let's begin with those. Let's assume that you want to say the word "Ah":

1. You can stop the breath before you begin by putting a glottal stop in front of the word or holding your breath "closed" before you say the word ("ah!" or "uh-'oh"). This is the word of surprise or warning. If you do this correctly, you start with a silence!

2. You can have breath flowing already, by putting an h at the beginning of the word (ha). If you do this correctly, your breath will already be moving before you make the note itself.

3. You can glide into the note without either breath or a stop by holding your breath "open" or "hovering" before you make the sound – (<ah). If you do this correctly, the sound and the breath happen together, and you get a very smooth start to the note – there's no sound of breath flowing already, and there's no sudden attack. This is in fact the one that classical singers use the most, because it's a smooth, gliding onset.

Now let's move to the pop and rock recording artists (and of course blues, soul, gospel, death metal, grunge – you get the picture…). Contemporary commercial music uses these three onsets, but they have much more fun using all sorts of new ones. Here's a few for you to play with:

4. Creak like an old door opening. You can sometimes find this if you talk like you are *really* tired. It's a gentle sound and can mean you are being very tired or deliberately sexy. If you do this correctly, your breath flow will be very small and slow, and the sound will "creak" into the note.
5. Flip onto the note. This means that you usually start the note higher and flip down onto the "real" note. The most extreme cases sound like Tarzan, but it depends how much higher you start. This is a favourite with Country and Western singers. If you do this correctly, it'll sound like a yodel or a "catch in the voice".
6. Squeeze the note. This is a more dangerous one (after all, that's what it's supposed to sound like). You start by aiming for the note in your head and squeezing it out of a tighter throat. The best version of this is to begin the note with the squeeze then open your throat quickly to get a clearer sound. If you do this correctly, you'll stay on the same note but start it with a more muffled, "strained" sound and open onto a clearer note straight away.

Here's a tip: onsets work best when the word starts with a vowel, but you *can* do them on words beginning with other letters. Start by using words such as "ah", "yeah", "oh", and "uh"

### *Make It Stop!*

And anything you can do to start a note, you can do to finish it. Experiment with these ideas:

- Sing a word and practise **ending** it with a creak.
- Do the same thing, ending with a flip.
- Now sing the same word and end with a squeeze.
- Have fun mixing and matching – start a note with a squeeze and end with a flip
- Now start *and* stop with a creak
- Start with breath flowing and end with a creak.

Now that you're getting the feel of these onsets and offsets, go back and listen to your favourite artist again. Remember that these onsets only happen at the very beginning of the note or phrase, and the offsets happen at the very end. Notice which onsets and offsets your singer uses.

In fact, they'll use some of the sounds you've just learned and not others. That's because their style includes certain things and excludes others, and they wouldn't want to change their style too much, or they might lose you as a fan.

Once you've found these onsets in your own voice, sing a few lines of your favourite artist's songs and experiment with using different onsets at the beginning of the phrases. When you copy the onsets and offsets they use, you start to sound much more like them.

* * *

## MOVING THE MALE VOICE FROM OPERA TO MUSICALS

I was working with a tenor last week who wanted to sing more show stuff. As an operatic singer, he has a bright, full lyric sound, and is used to singing Cavaradossi or Rodolfo (or even Verdi's Otello). However, he's a bit of a stranger to musical theatre, so it was an interesting session getting him to sing "Love Changes Everything" from *Aspects of Love.*

When I started coaching him in "Love Changes Everything", he was singing with the type of legato line and connected sound for the operatic genre. But it sounded wrong for musical theatre.

First, I asked him to do something that not all opera singers are used to… putting into the text all the commas, semicolons and full stops. This may be surprising to non-operatic singers, but opera singers are taught to produce a fully connected, continuous stream of sound.

Adding the punctuation started to break up the line, but the sounds were still too well matched. The problem here is that the listener focuses on the beautiful arching line instead of the song lyrics. In opera the emotion tends to come from the musical and emotional shapes of the phrases. In musical theatre, the emotion tends to come from the song lyrics, with the musical shapes coming second.

In addition, the song is a classic build song, it starts soft and just continues climbing to the big finish. Unless there is variation in the text and meaning, the singer ends up pushing vocally to top what he has started with. I've seen it happen so many times!

I asked him to add breath to the opening sounds, making the character seem (ironically) more breathless. Using a lot of breath in the sound means you must breathe more, and any singer worth his salt will then have to work out where to breathe that makes sense with the words. In operatic language, this made him come "off the voice" – he couldn't use the central core of tone that he normally has, as using breath interferes with the process.

The result from that one instruction was surprising, even by my standards. I had tingles listening to him, and all the hair stood up on the back of my neck. Those of you who know me (or have seen my photograph) know that this is no mean feat. As with many singers, if you give him a clear instruction, he follows it to the letter. He also said it was much easier to sing, and made the climax easier, bigger and more exciting.

Which leads me nicely into…

# COACHING CLASSICAL SINGERS – IT'S A DIFFERENT WORLD

Yes, classical singers are different to (and just as lovely as) musical theatre singers and contemporary commercial singers. Tonal quality and consistency are paramount, so we focus on sound in motion, linking imagination with voice, musical phrasing and structural architecture, and big emotional landscapes. Classical singers don't (officially) have access to microphones and sound systems, so they must still produce the level of volume and projection required for the concert hall or the opera house.

This collection contains some of my most recent work on imagination, gesture and imagery (all relevant to singers in any genre).

## THE SLIDE, THE SWING AND THE HICCUPS – IMAGERY IN ARIA COACHING

Those of you who know my work and the usual technical or musical precision of my instructions will perhaps raise an eyebrow at me using imagery in my singing coaching sessions. But today I was working with a new classical client and this fun session produced the swimming pool slide, the swing and the hiccups.

### *The Background*

My client arrives today with the classical arias "Vissi d'arte" and "Porgi, amor". Both are big arias in their way, divided by over 100 years of opera writing (1900 and 1786, respectively). This client has recently discovered a much bigger voice and is enjoying the exploration of more dramatic repertoire.

### *What Worked and What Needed to Change*

We start with the Tosca aria, "Vissi d'arte". The client has the voice for it, but the phrases feel "calculated" – all the notes are there but there is no real flow. The first change I want to make is to get her to move her voice around in a different way. The full lyric sopranos (bigger voices) that I've worked with connect notes in a very different way to my soubrettes.

### *Smearing*

I decide to use the smearing exercise. In this exercise you take a phrase and sing it very slowly. Full resonance on each note, then KEEP the resonance, tone and volume and slide (smear) your way slowly to the next note. Yes, you're essentially glissandoing between the notes – the point is to keep exactly the same vocal setup, sound, vibrato and breath flow on the *journey* between the notes, so that there is no real difference between the travelling to, and the arrival on, the target pitch.

Bear in mind that this isn't "hold the tone, back off and straighten to slide, then add the tone again". That just sounds like a truck making a three-point turn… In the smear version, there is no difference in setup, tone colour and volume when you're on the note or when you're moving between the notes.

This is an extremely effective exercise for vocal movement and phrasing. Once you have experienced this, you can decide whether you connect ALL the notes with a slow smear or whether you want to speed up the movement and make the listener believe you've "stepped" to the next note.

### *Imagery That Works*

The image/description to achieve this that works best for this client is a swimming pool slide. It gives her exactly the right amount of subglottal pressure, even volume and a sense of forward momentum without gripping or pushing. How did I know that? It was repeatable, and my client felt it was a lot easier and matched how she imagined herself singing. The sound that comes out is more vibrant, denser, used less breath and energy, and seems more appropriate to the writing and to Tosca's situation.

By the way, this is something else I look out for in my coaching sessions – when we hit the right balance for that *singer* with that *voice* singing that *aria* in that *context*, even supposedly difficult arias become easy and enjoyable for that singer to perform. And it's important not to impose my imagery (or the imagery that worked with the previous client) onto the singer in the room – it's *their* imagination that's important.

### *Dynamics and the Garden Swing*

The second bit of imagery relates to dynamics. In the middle of "Vissi d'arte" the phrases are marked *piano*. If you are wielding a big voice, it's easy to tighten up when you see the instruction to sing softly – your throat closes and you lose the tone quality. It's useful to remember that dynamics in singing are relative to the size of the voice and the repertoire (orchestration and drama). Because a bigger voice usually has a solid core to the tone, a *piano* sound will be bigger, denser and more present than the *piano* for a lighter-voiced soprano. To help my client find an easy piano for her voice, and more variation in her dynamics in general without sacrificing her tone colour, here are the instructions I use:

1. Sing the phrase "Nell'ora del dolore" etc at a healthy *mezzo forte* all the way through. Get comfortable, as this is your "ground

zero". Everything you sing in this exercise relates to this volume and tone colour.

2. Sing the phrase again starting at the same *mezzo forte* then go one notch louder.

3. Repeat going one notch quieter.

4. Repeat the phrase experimenting with 1, 2 or 3 notches louder or quieter, always starting from your "ground zero" *mezzo forte.*

The imagery that works for my client in this exercise is to imagine a garden swing. The swing in its still / balanced state represents *mezzo forte*. It could move in either direction (louder or softer) in relation to its still state.

The difference in her singing is remarkable. After one repetition of the above exercise she is more in control of volume, changing it at will without losing the richness of the sound or the feeling of supporting the tone. Again, she *felt* it was how she wanted to sing.

### *The Hiccups*

Figure 3: Excerpt from "Vissi d'arte", Tosca.

Finally, we focus on the phrases in the middle of the aria. "Sempre con fè sincera la mia preghiera ai santi tabernacoli salì. Sempre con fè sincera…". In these phrases there are three little grace notes, on fè, tabernacoli and fè. It's not unusual for some sopranos to gloss over these notes if they are not sure how to interpret what's written. There's a trick to learning grace notes like these, and it's in two parts:

1. Make sure to learn the pitch of the grace note. In the first phrase the fè is on a Bb but has a C grace note. That means you must pitch the vowel on the C (the consonant is an unvoiced f so can't be pitched). By adding this C to the note *before*, you get both the pitch and the approximate timing. So "con" becomes confè-è on Bb+C+Bb. Make sure to sing the è vowel on the C as well as the following Bb. This is more complex to write than to do! With "tabernacoli" the grace note is on the Bb, which is a minor third higher than the previous note. So the sung word for this part of the exercise becomes ta-berna-acoli, with the "na" pitched on the Bb. The same applies to the final "Sempre con fè sincera" – the phrase becomes "Sempre confè-è sincera" with the word confè-è sung on three notes (C+Eb+D).

2. In part 1 of this exercise you focused on singing the notes (and which part of the word is sung on the grace note) to let your voice and brain be accurate to the music. But it's dry and doesn't carry the appropriate information to the listener. You need a reason to sing them. Sing the phrase again and this time think of the grace note as being a little kick, or as my client said, an emotion hiccup. You will retain your pitch accuracy but now you have added meaning to the writing.

My client works on just these three phrases then sings the aria again. Because she now understands how the grace notes work and what to do, she automatically sings the two additional ones on "della Madonna al manto" and "che ne ridean piu belli" correctly without practising. Result!

The client is thrilled, and also slightly annoyed that no-one in her singing history has told her about these simple things before. Well, that's what you come to me for – simple and profound changes that make sense, work for your voice and help you express who you are as a singer.

* * *

## IMAGERY IN ARIA COACHING – BICYCLE WHEEL AND ESCALATOR

Following on from "The slide, the swing and the hiccups – imagery in aria coaching", my client has brought Porgi amor, from Mozart's *Marriage of Figaro*. It's a tricky aria at the best of times – it's the first thing the Countess sings and it's very slow and sustained. Add to that the fact that my client is singing with a voice that is bigger than she previously thought, and it becomes terrifying.

Here's how I coached her to feel in control of her sound and the aria.

### *Getting in the Groove*

We start (as I usually do) with a sing-through of the whole piece. It helps the singer feel comfortable, to get into the groove of performing, and it helps me discover where that singer's voice and energy is that day.

### *Sing With Your Own Voice*

Figure 4: "Porgi, amor", The Marriage of Figaro, excerpt 1.

Now to focus on the opening phrases. Even at a slow speed, these phrases aren't very long (just 2 or 3 bars each), but they do require a high level of control. She was bumping the opening note and then tightening to control the volume. Since we'd worked on the Tosca aria earlier in the session I encourage her to bring the garden swing technique we'd explored into the Mozart. It helps to sing the aria slightly bigger than you would expect so that you can "feel" how your voice works in this music at a decent volume. It is essential whatever music you are singing that you sing with your own voice, and that sometimes means singing / feeling / hearing the phrases with a louder connected volume than you would use for a performance.

### *The Bicycle Wheel*

Since this client responds so well to imagery my mind comes up with the bicycle wheel. Imagine putting your finger on the top rim of the wheel, pushing it round and arriving back at the top. The arrival point is the top, and the bottom of the wheel is a point that you travel *through*.

How does this apply to "Porgi, amor"? I notice that the arrival point in each of the first three 2-bar phrases is the beginning of the *second* bar, not the first. By seeing the opening note as an "already travelling through" point and starting "at the bottom of the wheel" my client can sing the phrase without the opening bump and move through to the second bar.

That simple change has so many knock-on effects. She is able to control the opening note of the aria very effectively without closing her throat; each phrase has a sense of travelling forwards (this aria is notorious for slowing down); and because the forward momentum is now built into the phrasing, she is able to sustain the phrases easily so could sing it realistically at a slower speed. And since each phrase rises and falls like a sigh, she can reflect that emotion just by using the *travel–arrive–travel again* feel of the bicycle wheel.

This even works for the next set of phrases – three bars each – and the climbing phrase to the Ab.

There's a hilarious moment in the lesson when we notice the next phrases are like little trainer wheels – 2 semiquavers each ("Porgi amor qual che ristoro al mio duolo a miei sospir"), then back to the 2-bar circle.

### ***The Escalator***

Figure 5: "Porgi, amor", The Marriage of Figaro, excerpt 2.

The next tricky bit is the rising phrase over a ninth on "lascia". The bicycle wheel didn't feel appropriate for this as it's a smooth climb. So we "step onto the escalator" for the rising ninth scale. This works surprisingly well. In real life, the escalator does all the work of carrying you up, so there was no sense of driving up to the top note. Having arrived at the high G, we use the idea of arriving at the top of the escalator before you expect to, to reflect the curious offbeat rhythm pattern in the phrase (you stagger a little as you go from assisted climbing to flat floor walking).

That is a particularly bizarre image to play with, but again, it works brilliantly for my client. She now has a real sense of ease in the phrase, the sound and emotion match the writing, and the piece loses its terror.

She sings the aria through using this imagery and it's like listening to a different singer. My client is happy, and I'm fascinated by the way that each singer's brain works in conjunction with their voice. I'm looking forward to the next session!

*If you want to know what I can do to help your singing feel easier and more authentic, come and work with me in person or online – I'd love to help you discover more about your voice and performing.*

* * *

## FIVE QUICK AND EASY STEPS TO LEARNING RECITATIVE

This is a variation on my "Learn a Song in 15 Minutes" sequence (see above), with a slant towards operatic recitative.

Recitative comprises music that is written in the style of ordinary speech. It appears in operas from Caccini to Mozart and even Stravinsky, and in church music including Gregorian chant and Bach's cantatas.

Many young singers I have worked with think of recitative in opera as the filler between the important bits and can tend to gloss over it to get to the meaty arias or duets. But it is usually there to carry the plot forwards and can be a highly emotional experience.

Recitative can hold some terrors for the young (and even the experienced) singer, as its rhythmic and melodic structures often differ from the surrounding music. Singers are musicians at heart, and the temptation is to start with the melody and throw the words in somehow. But this takes longer to do, and you are more likely to make mistakes that are difficult to undo.

Here are five simple steps I use in my coaching to help singers read, understand and learn recitative. The sample Italian recitative comes from "Come scoglio", Fiordiligi's aria in Mozart's *Così fan tutte*. You can view the complete score online at
http://www.dlib.indiana.edu/variations/scores/scores.html

1. Start with the words, in whatever language it is written. Read them through aloud, listening for accurate vowels, and looking for odd pronunciations or strings of unusual letters. In Italian, several words are often strung together resulting in three or four vowels in a row – make sure you know and can pronounce all of them.
   *"Temerari, sortite fuori di questo loco"*
   [If you have a word-for-word translation, use it now only to get the flavour of the emotions you are portraying: *"You reckless man, leave here immediately"*
2. Now read the words aloud again, but this time emphasize every syllable that moves pitch. Although this might feel odd (and unmusical), it is in fact the most important part of the process. It will enable you to discover on which word the pitch movements really occur. And even though you are not yet singing, your brain is already learning the shapes of the phrases.
   *"Te-MEra-RI, SOR ti-TE FUOri di quesTO LO-CO*
3. Now go to the melody, and hum or "ng" your way through it. You are looking / listening / feeling for the arch or shape of the phrase, and the tonality. Don't worry if you can't play the piano or put the chords in underneath what you are singing – it's enough to understand the shape. If you do play the piano or can think harmonically, notice where the tonality or chord changes and emphasize that too.
4. Now put the words and melody together, taking time to emphasize the words where the pitch moves. Again, this helps you to embed precisely where things change (as opposed to where they stay on the same note).

5. Finally, look for the long notes in each phrase. Most classic recitative is written in quavers (eighth notes), so look out for crotchets (quarter notes) or minims (half notes), and be sure to put them in. The long notes will give you the rhythmic structure of the sentence the composer wants. In this example, the first syllable of *TEmerari* is the longest note in the phrase. You don't need to pay too much attention to long notes at the ends of phrases – they are often put there by editors trying to fill the bar.

The trick to learning recitative is to consciously identify the patterns and shapes in the words and the music. Once you have discovered exactly where the different patterns start, you can use them as hooks to speed through the non-moving sections. I recommend that you do steps 1 to 5 at a slower (thinking) speed. Once you have completed those steps, you will find that you are able to sing the recitative confidently and effectively at speed.

And if you don't believe me, just try it!

* * *

You may be wondering why the next piece is written in the third person. I'm not trying to big myself up by referring to an alter ego called "Fisher", it's a piece written by journalist Josette Lesser published by the sadly now defunct *Singer* magazine. "K" was looking for help on acting coaching as an opera singer for auditioning, so Josette sat in on our hour-long session. This is an excerpt from the resulting article.

## ACTING IN OPERA – THE *SINGER MAGAZINE* SITS IN ON A COACHING CLASS BY JEREMY FISHER.

Fisher starts his class with K by discussing her requirements. He then gives her the option of talking through the audition set-up or singing and experiencing it. When she admits that she's an intellectualiser,

Fisher tells her to sing! The piece she chooses is "Pace, pace mio Dio" from Verdi's *La Forza del Destino*. After her first rendition, Fisher gives her feedback: "The first thing I see is that you're not completely committed. I can see why somebody would say that the emotions don't come across. It's not true that you're not doing the emotions. You are. I want to work with you on doing something completely different with it, because I think that you've got an image of what this person is, should be, behaves like."

He also points out that, although the music is very static, emotionally it is heartfelt and powerful. He asks her to pace up and down and work entirely against the music. "Sing it exactly the same," he instructs, "but physically you're going to be really frustrated, fraught, angry, fiery, hyper."

The difference is immediately apparent: "It's a question of not going with what you think you should be doing and going with something that fits you" he explains. "We've got to take you and put you into the character, not the other way around. And sometimes you have to go to the other extreme to find something of yours that you can bring in."

Fisher asks what the aria is about, and as the discussion deepens, it is clear that he is going to make K use every ounce of her own, very outgoing personality: "Victims don't suit you" he declares. He gets her to analyze the words victim and passive, slowly leading her to the idea of an active, boxed-in character: "I think your image of victim is: Not dealing with the situation. And I think you're going: This is not what I do. I can sing the notes, I can do the phrases, I'm musical, but I don't have any resonance with that character. So for you, character-wise, were going to use a slightly different version: she's frustrated as hell and she fights. Let me die! – frustration is a very hot, angry emotion. Passive isn't hot, but by moving you around were already getting some of the heat of: I am in a terrible situation and I can't do anything about it. It's about putting your sense of drama into what you're doing."

However, drama and emotion are all very well but, as we well know, they should never affect the quality of one's singing. Fisher's solution to this is to fake the emotion: "Ultimately your job is to make us feel it", he tells her. "I don't care if you feel it. In fact, if you did feel it and let your singing down, I'd be really annoyed. So that's your job as an actor in any shape or form."

By the end of the session he has also covered everything from biting into the voiced consonants for extra effect, to reviewing the actual audition procedure. And the difference in K's performance is quite remarkable. Afterwards I asked her how she felt? "It was exactly what I was looking for!" she enthuses, "I came away elated and optimistic that Jeremy could help me move towards where I want to be. His combination of theoretical knowledge and practical exercises impressed me, combined with obvious musical ability – well, who could ask for anything more? I've come away with a lot to think about, practical things I can do to improve my performing, not just theories. My brain is humming, and so am I."

*"Just what we at The Singer like to hear. Next query."*

* * *

## ARE YOU TALKING TO ME?

I have just read a fascinating article by the excellent performance coach Noa Kageyama on self-talk. His website bulletproofmusician.com is a great resource for singers and performers. Noa is extremely good at taking the latest scientific research on performance and breaking it down into understandable language and do-able suggestions. I've been on his mailing list for years and always enjoy his take on performing.

https://bulletproofmusician.com/gain-a-psychological-edge-by-talking-about-yourself-in-the-third-person/

The original researchers at Michigan University ran seven studies on the language people use to refer to themselves, and how that language influences how they think, feel and behave under stress.

They found that "using non-first-person pronouns and one's own name (rather than first-person pronouns) during introspection enhances self-distancing." So referring to myself as "you", "he" and "Jeremy" when I'm processing events or analysing what just happened enables me to examine potentially disturbing events without getting as emotionally involved.

This is really useful for practising, as you can appraise your singing with less negative emotions and more practical advice for yourself.

Jeremy does this a lot when learning new pieces and he thinks it's an excellent idea.

* * *

## CORE TONE FOR KEEPS?

This section follows on from previous articles on style and genre differences:

One thing that matters to opera singers is keeping the core tone throughout the phrase and not to "disappear" at the end. This is a big topic for non-classical singers (incidentally, the latest phrase is Contemporary Commercial Music or CCM singers). Most CCM plays on a singer's ability to differentiate between registers and voice qualities, and sound decay is used a great deal. It is rare (except perhaps in Gospel) for the same volume and intensity to be maintained throughout a phrase or a song. Particularly in pop, R&B and soul, the vocal phrases tend to follow the shape of the sentence, so notes at the ends of phrases will fade, fall away or be cut short.

Now before all you opera singers start emailing me in disgust (again), yes, I know that there is shaping and "phrasing" in classical music. However, the scale of it is smaller than in, say, a song performed by Blue. In fact, the whole architecture differs between a CCM song and an operatic aria, particularly in later 19th-century opera. One of the basic tenets of classical singing is that there is "line" and "tone" all the time. Any deviation from this is just that, a deviation. If you listen to the number of changes of quality and interrupted line that occur in any Blue song, you begin to realize that changing musical genres is more than just changing your sound.

### *From Jazz to Opera*

"We have to reproduce faithfully what's on the page in classical music". Opera star Renée Fleming on the radio show *Desert Island Discs.*

Well, yes and no – it depends. What standard musical notation doesn't show you is how to move between the notes. When singers are discovering a new musical genre, they sometimes need a little help!

I often work with classically trained singers who want to widen their choice of working styles. But this week I was working with a singer / teacher who has travelled from the opposite direction. She is a fairly accomplished jazz / blues singer who has just discovered a classical setup. It's a big voice! We're working on full lyric repertoire, and it's been interesting to note that for her, the change of vocal setup makes her feel that her voice is freer and more powerful, although the sheer size of the noise scares her a little.

Ironically, when she came for the session, she was singing exactly what was on the page, moving cleanly from note to note (like a conscientious instrumentalist). I had to explain to her that big lyric voices, particularly in operatic repertoire, tend to move between the notes in a different way to singers in other genres. So I have had her sliding between the notes, singing through phrases on a voiced fricative (vv), and generally connecting notes and pitches without the words. She certainly found it easier to sing the repertoire (Countess, Tosca, even French song).

This repertoire needs the singer to add connection between the notes, slides (supported smearing between the pitches), and linking shapes, together with a much bigger arching shape in the phrase.

### *Core Tone*

The other thing that matters is keeping the "core tone" throughout the phrase, and not disappearing at the ends of phrases. One definition of maintaining core tone is that the sound stays focused and alive and remains present even when getting softer. If you're a classical singer, that's one of those "but of course" moments.

But to someone new to the genre, particularly a singer who is used to creating widely differing sounds within a phrase, that's a surprise.

As this singer said to me: "Do you mean I have to do that ALL THE TIME?"

* * *

## 97 OPERAS THAT NEVER MADE IT

Just before we leave the world of opera coaching and crossover, here are 97 opera titles that didn't quite make the grade

Opera composers are busy people, but sometimes they don't get the title quite right the first time. If you're an opera fan, how many of these operas do you know without looking them up? If you can name all 97 of them correctly, award yourself one Puccini.

1. Bartok: Bluebeard's End Terrace (with off-street parking)
2. Beethoven: Infidelio
3. Bellini: Abnorma (the subject of a Channel 5 documentary)
4. Bellini: Il Piranha (starring Marina Callous)
5. Bellini: Norman
6. Berg: Catsick
7. Berg: Lu
8. Berg: Wozzup?
9. Berlioz: Beatrice et Benedictine (the sorry tale of a love that tippled over into addiction)
10. Bizet: Les pêcheurs de prawns
11. Bizet: Vanmen
12. Britten: Diaorrhea in Venice
13. Britten: Noye's Incontinence
14. Britten: The Turn of the IKEA fitment
15. Busoni: Trainee Nurse Faust (the doktor will be along shortly)
16. Catalani: Where's Wally
17. Debussy: Pelleas and his smelly sandals
18. Delius: The Village Romeo and Julian
19. Donizetti: Excretia Bogeya
20. Donizetti: L'Elisir de vague interest
21. Donizetti: Lendus di Chamouleather
22. Donizetti: Maria's Too Hard (the stirring tale of a prizewinning Scottish female boxer)
23. Donizetti: Spag Bolena
24. Dvorak: Rusalkaselzer
25. Gershwin: Porky and Butch
26. Gluck: Iphigenie in Torremolinos
27. Handel: Semoline
28. Handel: Tamburino

29. Hindemith: Cardillac Arrest
30. Humperdinck: Hans Werner Henze und Gretel
31. Janáček: Katya KabtoBrixton
32. Janáček: The Cunning Little Gerbil
33. Johann Strauss II: Die Fledersquirrel
34. Krenek: Jonny Spielt Banjo
35. Lehar: Land of Smirks
36. Leoncavallo: Caballero Rusticanopener (the horsemeat scandal)
37. Leoncavallo: Listen Pal…
38. Massenet: Donkey Shot
39. Massenet: Silk Thaïs
40. Maxwell Davies: Eight Songs For A Mad Baritone
41. Menotti: Amahl and the Night Visitors and the Social Worker and the Registered List
42. Menotti: The iPhone
43. Menotti: The XXL
44. Meyerbeer: What's that din (or Pardon My French)
45. Monteverdi: L'Incontinenzione di Poppea
46. Mozart: Cozzie, fan, tutu (an opera about ballet)
47. Mozart: Die Zauberbanjo
48. Mozart: Le Nose di Figaro (It's in for a long run)
49. Mozart: Mitridate, re di Pontypridd
50. Mozart: The UnimpressAria
51. Mussorgsky: Boris Reasonablunov
52. Offenbach: Les Tweets D'Hoffmann
53. Prokofiev: Love For A Satsuma
54. Prokofiev: The Duennythingforcash
55. Puccini: Candied Angelica
56. Puccini: La Fan Chiller del West End (air-conditioned theatres)
57. Puccini: PerDiem (Touring Dough)
58. Puccini: Tosser
59. Reimann: Leer (a king with a roving eye)
60. Richard Strauss: Ariadne auf Neasden
61. Richard Strauss: Der Pansykavalier
62. Richard Strauss: Die Frau ohne Scheissen
63. Richard Strauss: Salame
64. Richard Strauss: The Talking Woman (well, the Silent Woman is mythological…)

65. Rimsky-Korsakov: KönigskinderSurprise (there's a hidden toy inside each one)
66. Rossini: FakeTancredi
67. Rossini: Fullyramide
68. Rossini: Il Turdo in Italia
69. Rossini: Il Viaggio a Romford
70. Rossini: La Cenebuytoletola (following the demise of the rental market)
71. Rossini: Mose is an Eedjit (a great tenor role)
72. Rossini: Semidetachedramide
73. Rossini: The Thieving Tit
74. Saint-Saëns: Samsung and the Lilo (the perfect opera for the beach)
75. Shostakovich: Snot
76. Sondheim: Onis Todd
77. Stravinsky: The Fire Extinguisher Bird (Health and Safety)
78. Sullivan: HMRC Pinafore (investigation pending)
79. Tchaikovsky: YouGin? OneGin!
80. Thomas: Cheese and Ham Omelet
81. Verdi: The Hilton Otello (a place to lay your head)
82. Verdi: The Sicilian Vespa (fast, economical and stylish)
83. Verdi: Travelodgeo (it's a second class Otello)
84. Verdi: Un disco in papier maschera
85. Wagner: Damntheguttering
86. Wagner: Longandgrim
87. Wagner: Siegincarcerated
88. Wagner: The Flying Dutchcap
89. Wagner: Tristan and 'is older sister
90. Walton: Sir John in't Loo
91. Weber: Der Freiup
92. Weill: Jonny Spits it Out
93. Weill: Miserable End
94. Weill: The Rise and Fall of the City of MDF
95. Weill: The Seven Deadly Singers
96. Wolf-Ferrari: Ill secretion di Susanna
97. Zandonai: Francesca da Royston Vasey

The next section tells the story of a singer-pianist who came to me for three sessions to improve his performing. Singers who play instruments have special issues to deal with, and I love troubleshooting with these particular vocal musicians. It's also surprising how many of the problems instrumentalists have are relevant to all singers.

# COACHING THE SINGER-PIANIST

I LOVE doing this. As a singer-pianist myself I have – literally – hands-on experience of the joys and woes of singing from the keyboard. Pianistic technique? Check. Split brain? Check. Sell the lyrics of a song while providing complex harmonies? Check.

Singer-instrumentalists out there, I want to work with you!

## COACHING THE SINGER-PIANIST: WHAT DO THEY TEACH THEM AT COLLEGE?

I have been working with a singer-pianist recently. It's reminded me how different it is to work with an instrumentalist. For those singers among you who are about to bombard me with rude emails, let me explain. The majority of singers come to the art form late, precisely because of the massive physical changes that happen to their instrument in teenage.

Most instrumentalists have already started their training before teenage (I began playing piano when I was 6), and usually have a fairly solid background in the theory and practice of music. That means the language I can use in my coaching sessions changes.

In fact, the whole business of learning music is a fascinating one, and for me it is important to delineate between different genres of music. Anyone who has talked to me or read any of my publications knows that I tend to separate classically trained singers and theatre or pop singers. This is not to do with the training, this is to do with the purpose of the music they sing. I deal on a weekly basis with singers wanting to cross the genres, and the following information often comes as a shock to someone who has devoted much of their training to one musical genre.

Classical singers are taught line, phrasing, matching sounds and arcs of vocal shape. Text and storyline come second to matching beautiful tone. (We still have 45-year-old women of a certain weight playing a teenage fragile consumptive, or 60-year-old tenors singing student roles, because it's the voice that counts). Opera tends to work with mythology, or "grand design" plots, and recital music tends to focus on the poetic and formal. Classical music can have a long shelf life because of its reliance on legends and historical stories. In fact, when a classical singer gets to sing non-serious topics, it gets called "On the lighter side". [Love the singers, *hate* the phrase.]

Musical theatre singers are usually actors first, and so are taught text and characterization. The singing and the vocal sounds arise from the needs of the text and storyline. (We still have actors who find it tricky to sing in tune being cast in "singing" roles, because it's the characterization and the physical casting that counts.)

Musical theatre deals with mythology more rarely, but will tackle contemporary issues such as racism, physical and social diseases and segregation of all kinds. Musical theatre has a mid-term shelf life: musicals can have revivals but are often updated during the process.

Pop and contemporary commercial singers use "street language", extreme but everyday feelings (e.g. teenage and hormone-driven) and repetition to carry their message, so recognizable emotion is the most important thing. (We still have singers in their late 20s with children of their own, performing at the bottom or top of their fully-developed range in songs aimed at pre-teens, because it's the image and the feeling that counts.) Much of this music is instantly recognizable (and disposable) because it appeals to the immediate. You could say that this music, rather than taking you out of yourself, takes you into yourself, to help you identify and accept (or reject) the feelings you are enduring. This musical genre (or genres) also has the most tribal background, with million-strong fan bases. OK, now you can send me emails…

### *Coaching the Singer-Pianist: A Balancing Act*

So back to the singer-pianist. He's been working on his voice with Gillyanne and has come to me for some sessions on integrating singing and playing. Coaching singer-pianists is one of my favourite things to do. They are usually good musicians open to new ideas. As I have intimate knowledge and a muscle awareness of the trials and joys of playing for my own singing, it's interesting to see how other people cope with the problems.

He's an excellent pianist and can be heard playing at major London hotels like the Lanesborough. He has a smooth bass voice and can switch between jazz standards and comedy patter songs, so is pretty versatile. The problems: balancing voice and piano (the usual one), diction and projection (with and without the mike). I suggested that he began by rebalancing the piano playing. Solo pianists tend to amplify the upper right hand, so that the melody shines out above everything else. Accompanists can't afford to do that, as the melody is usually allotted to someone else. In my own case (and I am an accompanist or collaborative pianist by training and by inclination), I emphasize the lower left hand, to create a solid foundation for the rest of the harmonies. This means that you can make the right-hand harmonies more transparent yet get a richer sound. Rebalancing like this will mean that the voice is supported from underneath (yes, even a bass voice), without too much going on in the same pitch range to blur the sound. Although this is a bit of a brainpain to begin with for him, the effect is pretty instant – his voice begins to come to the fore, and he "gets it" that vocal life becomes easier.

### *Coaching the Singer-Pianist: Diction*

Continuing the session with the singer-pianist. His diction is good, although his voice quality is a little too gentle and "defocused" to truly carry. Rather than change the voice quality, I work with him on upping the diction.

There are two ways to create clearer diction as far as I am concerned: louder consonants or longer consonants. The first version is well-known, and I see a number of singers in my studio who have been told to "spit the consonants". Personally, I think this is only useful in extreme circumstances. I prefer the second alternative, elongation.

In order to elongate consonants, you must know where they are made. Each consonant is a partial or complete obstruction, and each obstruction happens in a specific place. A *b* is bi-labial – both lips come together to block the exit of air momentarily. Incidentally, your nose is also closed in a *b*; if it wasn't, you'd have an *m*!

A *v* uses the top teeth against the bottom lip. The *v* is a good example of how a consonant might be "spat". Most singers when told to emphasize a *v* will simply bite harder between the lip and teeth to produce more back pressure in the mouth and throat. This can be painful, although it can produce a louder sound temporarily.

Since all consonants are essentially cues to the audience that something is happening to the vowel, there is a much easier way to emphasize the *v*. By elongating the cue (the sound of the airflow travelling through the gap made between the touching lip and teeth) but not increasing it with speed or volume, the audience picks up that the consonant is a *v* without you having to work as hard. You are starting it earlier in the bar and singing it longer. The partial obstruction is there (the lip to the teeth) and does not need to be exaggerated – the simple act of holding the sound longer will create the emphasis. Try it out yourself.

Again, this is a coordination thing, and can cause a bit of brainpain when you first try it out, but it is amazing how crisp diction becomes when the movements are made precisely and without pressure, and then elongated for distance hearing. Life becomes so much easier. There is another gain, as my client pointed out. When you are working with a microphone, the last thing you want is spitting consonants – they'll pop the mike. The elongation works well for clarity without force.

### *Coaching the Singer-Pianist: Using Your Tongue*

Once the diction and balance of voice and piano were in place, there was really only one thing left to tackle in the first session: tongue use.

It became obvious to me as a listener that this client was backing his tongue when he sang. I listened carefully to his speaking voice, and there was very little backing in his own accent. I surmised that he was adding it to his singing for a reason.

Backing the tongue happens when the entire tongue is drawn backwards slightly. The sound becomes slightly "bottled" and the tone darker, as the oral pharynx (the back of the mouth space behind the tongue) becomes partly blocked. Incidentally, this is slightly different from singing with a low, flat tongue, where the blade sits low and flat in the mouth, ostensibly to give "space" in the oral cavity (in my experience, the intention and the reality don't necessarily coincide).

Backing the tongue usually happens with more inexperienced singers, as for some reason the tongue position allows you to hear more of the sound yourself (and less is let out to the listener). To you it sounds richer and warmer, but to us it sounds muffled and duller.

I had the feeling (confirmed by the client) that he wanted to hold back a little from giving his voice out. I told him it had the effect of drawing curtains around himself and hiding from the onlookers. That was a pretty effective image for him, and one he wanted to change, so we experimented with a different placement for his tongue. I suggested that he think of his tongue as a drawer on runners, and to slide the entire tongue backwards and forwards along his teeth. As he brought his tongue forwards by millimetres, the effect was instant. He was able to produce a clearer sound yet keep the diction. In addition, he was able to access edgy brightness easily, so his sound became more focused, brighter and with a great deal more presence. Now his playing and singing were much more balanced – his voice was "forward" and, coupled with the diction, gave him much more presence as a performer. He commented that everything seemed less effort, including the higher notes.

* * *

While I was putting this book together I found a group of articles that don't quite fit into any previous categories. I wanted to include them because they give a different perspective on what goes on in the brain of a vocal coach, so the next section includes all of them plus stories of some of the weird auditions *I've* done.

# STRANGE THINGS I'VE DONE

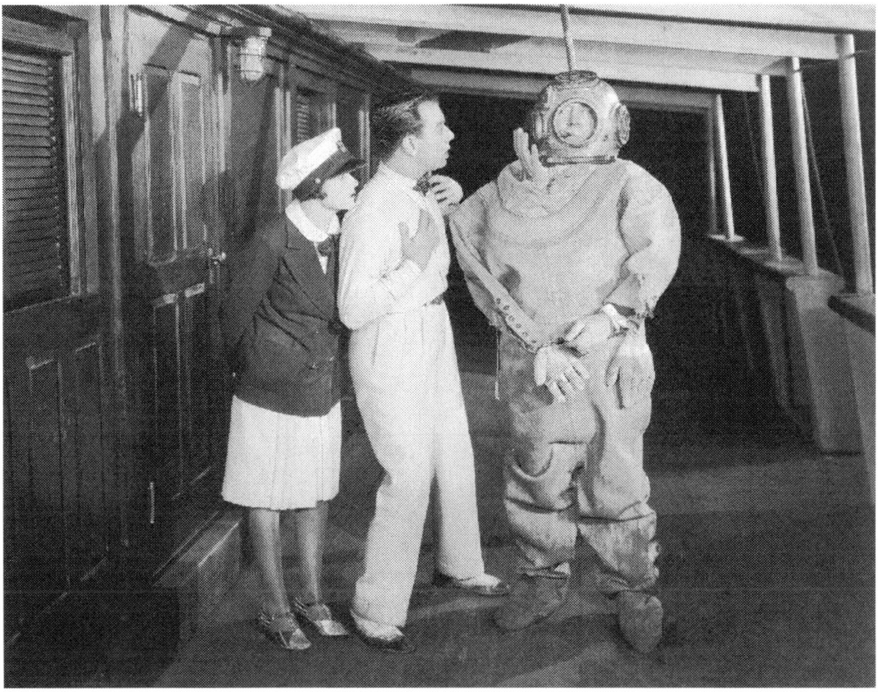

## CHUTZPAH AND MY FIRST PROFESSIONAL AUDITION

My first professional audition came about in a rather strange way. I had just spent 6 years of my life at the Royal Northern College of Music, studying oboe, then piano, then accompaniment, and was very successful at what I did. But when I left college, I had no job to go to, and very few prospects of concerts, despite being a prize-winning accompanist.

I looked around for jobs that might suit my particular brand of skills.

> *Skills:* Love working with singers, excellent sight-reader, interested in the theatre.
>
> *Me:* Hey, I'll become an opera repetiteur.

I rang Opera North, the nearest professional opera company, in Leeds

(I was in Manchester at the time). And I swear the following conversation is word for word what was said:

> *Me:* Hello, I'm a wonderful pianist, and you simply must employ me.
>
> *Opera North:* Yes dear, send us your CV and we'll audition you in 20 years' time or when someone dies.

I put the phone down, thinking, what a great answer – I'll do it.

I sent my CV (resumé) and didn't hear a thing for about 6 months. Then I had a phone call from Sheffield Crucible theatre saying that Opera North had recommended me as a good pianist, and they needed a rehearsal pianist for the UK Premiere of *Carmen Jones*, would I like to audition for the musical director?

When I arrived in Sheffield, the musical director, Jeremy Sams, met me at the stage door and took me to a dressing room. No piano, but that didn't seem to bother him. I talked a bit about what I had done at college, then asked if he wanted to hear me play.

> No, it's OK. You won the same prize that I did, so I know what standard you are. You've got the job.

And I hadn't played a note to anyone.

As it happened, I couldn't do the first day of rehearsals, so I arrived on the second day and the first thing I had to do was transpose the Toreador's song down a tone into Eb minor. Have you ever tried playing it? It's somewhat fiddly. And the second thing I had to do was play the Gypsy Dance ("Beat Out Dat Rhythm on a Drum") down a *fourth* at sight. At the end of the day I thought I had better resign before they sacked me. Fortunately, I went to lie down until the feeling wore off.

Needless to say, I can now play both of those pieces in both keys without breaking sweat. It just goes to show that sometimes you have no idea how well you are doing. And sometimes it doesn't matter how hard you work, the casting decisions are out of your hands.

*   *   *

## MY SECOND PROFESSIONAL AUDITION

Having been recommended by Opera North (who had never heard me play) to The Crucible Theatre, I finally got the call for an audition with Opera North. I was staying with friends in London and got a message on my pager (remember those? That shows how ooooold I am). Again, I swear this is what was paged to me:

> *Opera North:* We want you to audition for us on Thursday morning at 10am, you'll be working for us at 10.30.

Hey, looks like I can't go wrong with this, although you must admit it's a little bizarre. Now at the time I didn't know this, but an opera audition usually requires the pianist to play some arias or ensembles and to sightread an opera score (the piano reduction, not the orchestral score). Anyway, I didn't have a piano to practise on, and I was much too shy (yes really) to find a studio or hire a piano.

I researched what the company was working on that season, and decided to play "Batti, batti" from Mozart's *Don Giovanni*. I don't know if you know it, but there's a slightly tricky left hand, which represents the cello solo. I had played it several times before when I was at college and thought I could manage it quite well.

I was living in Leeds at the time in an unheated garret (no, I'm not kidding, I've done the poor musician in a garret bit. In fact, I'm wondering when it's going to end...). I got the *Don Giovanni* score out of the local library. Unfortunately for me, with no piano (and not thinking to look through the piece) I had got not the easy to play Schirmer piano reduction but the impossibly difficult Bärenreiter piano reduction, that just puts virtually every note the orchestra plays onto a piano stave.

Come the morning of the audition, and the senior conductor Clive Timms is waiting to hear me play. I launch into "Batti batti" and stop playing –

15 times in the first three pages.

The 15th time I actually say out loud, "Oh for heaven's sake, Fisher, pull yourself together!" This audition was fast going down the toilet.

Clive very gently said, "Yes, it is a little tricky, isn't it? Let's do some sightreading." He put the score of Gounod's *Faust* in front of me and started conducting.

Now there's one thing I can do, and that's sightread. Particularly 19th-century romantic stuff. I didn't bat an eyelid (or make a mistake, as I remember) and we sightread through the whole of Act 1 of *Faust*. I got the job.

Not that it got any less scary, as one of the first things I did was to play in the pit in front of the entire company for the first stage and piano rehearsal. I think Clive saw my face (terrified) when I realized I would be playing The Jewel Song (a favourite piece) for Valerie Masterson (a favourite singer) and rescued me. Just goes to show that making errors in an audition situation can still get you the job – but only if you recover fast!

* * *

## THE STORY OF MY WEST END DEBUT

I had an email a couple of days ago from a fellow pianist wanting to know how I got into the West End business in the first place. I'll be copying you in on my response a little later, but in the meanwhile, here's the story of my West End debut.

My very first job was 8 months understudying on *The Sneeze*, a series of 8 Chekhov plays with a cast headed by Rowan Atkinson and Timothy West. I was covering the performances and doing the understudy rehearsals every week. I had told the producers very early on that they simply weren't paying me enough money to sit in the theatre every night waiting to see if the pianist turned up. Instead, I would ring the theatre at 6.45 each evening, and 1.45 on matinee days, to see if I was needed.

Well, the eight months came and went, and nothing happened. In the last week of the run, we had our end-of-run party on the Thursday night after the show in a posh West End club. It was Russian-themed with vodka and Russian food and was very exciting to someone newly arrived in London.

The next day I was actually in the local sauna, and at 6.45 I thought I'd better get out and ring the theatre.

Yes, you're on tonight, Michael's got food poisoning.

At first, I thought they were joking – it was April Fool's day after all – but they were deadly serious, so I threw on my clothes and ran to the theatre. Of course, the tubes were crowded and of course I arrived late, but they had held the curtain for me and made an announcement to the audience.

I ran across the stage, into the box and started playing the show, too frazzled to be nervous. Apparently, Timothy West said *"Oh, he's rather good, isn't he?"* After all, he had never heard me play! All went well until the play *The Sneeze*, which is a silent play to Russian-style ballet music. I loved playing this music, and I did extremely well until the last two pages.

Apparently, I took the music rather faster than Michael played it, and everyone on the side of the stage watched as Rowan had to fairly throw himself around the stage to fit in all the business. I'm glad to say that I got a big ovation at the end. In fact, some of the cast thought it was a setup between me and Michael to give me a chance to play the show before it ended, but as I pointed out to them, if I'd known I was to play that night, I wouldn't have been in the sauna!

* * *

## AUDITIONING FOR *LES MISÉRABLES*

Getting the job on the West End production of *Les Misérables* was another of those odd occurrences that have happened in my life. One of my mezzo friends had asked me to play for her *Les Mis* audition. She was singing "I Was a Constant Faithful Wife" from Walton's *The Bear* and was doing auditions for *Les Mis* and for *Phantom of the Opera.*

The piece is more suitable for *Phantom*, really, but she decided to do it for both. If you don't know the piece, it's got an oom-chah accompaniment with a few twiddles in it and lots of pompous, over-the-top atmosphere. We did the *Les Mis* audition in the Palace Theatre and the MD called up from the stalls

> Thank you very much. Nice playing.

I was quite surprised, because the piano part isn't exactly spectacular, but I thought I'd make the most of the comment. So I stood at the stage door and wrote him a note…

> I'm the pianist of whom you said, 'Nice playing'. I'm a superb sightreader, so if you ever need a rehearsal or audition pianist, just let me know. Here's my phone number.

Well, 6 weeks later I had a phone call from the company manager:

> Did you mean it when you said you were a superb sightreader?
>
> Yes.
>
> OK, we'd like you to play for a rehearsal of the show on Thursday.

I presented myself on Thursday (having picked up a score and read it through beforehand) and delighted the director by knowing where the Cart Scene was before he even told me.

There are two morals here for budding professionals. Do your research (read the score and learn the story), and take advantage of anything that offers itself (keep a pen and paper handy for on-the-spot letters of introduction)

* * *

## STANDING OVATIONS AND *LES MISÉRABLES*

I remember playing in *Les Misérables* a few years ago. I had been the rehearsal and audition pianist on the show in the West End for years, and was head-hunted to take on the "Keyboard 1" part on the national tour. For those of you who don't know the show, it lasts three and a quarter hours (all but four characters are dead by the end – it's a fun evening). Doing eight shows a week and two rehearsals calls for a fair amount of stamina.

Now I don't know about the arrangement that's in the West End now, but in the original version, keyboard 1 plays the entire show. And I mean the entire show.

There are four volumes of music to play through each performance. In Act 2 there are two breaks, and the second one used to be just long enough to swivel 360 degrees (I was on a typist's chair) and start playing again. Of course, the best show was when the barricades got stuck. That means just one thing for the musicians – overtime!

*Les Misérables* is such an extraordinary show, and we used to get standing ovations every night. After about 6 weeks of this, we started to judge how well the show had gone, depending on how long it took the front row of the audience to stand up. Less than 3 seconds was a good show, more than about 6 seconds and it was definitely dodgy. The human brain can get used to anything, even success.

# THINGS THEY DON'T TEACH YOU AT COLLEGE

## THE REALITY OF LIFE ON THE ROAD

I'm back at a major music conservatoire next week to work with the new intake of BA students. And it started me thinking about the practical things that I *wasn't* taught at music college.

One topic came up last night in our Hatstand Opera "Bite At The Opera" performance at the Tenby Festival: How to rehearse in a new space.

Many students coming out of music college assume that how they sing is how they sing, and that's all there is to it. But they are completely missing the point of live performance, and the focus of the onsite rehearsal. For me the point of an onsite rehearsal isn't to practise the things you *should* already know, but don't. It's to begin working together as a group that day towards a common goal, to tweak anything that needs tweaking, and to find the good and bad points about the space you are working in. In fact, every time you move to a different location, you have a different set of acoustical problems to deal with.

Hatstand Opera is known as the "go anywhere" opera company, and since we don't normally work with a sound system, we carry our own acoustics with us. We have to deal with different spaces and acoustics almost every performance.

Last night, the stunning St Brides Spa Hotel in Saundersfoot, South Wales was our venue, in a beautiful though tricky space – a long, fairly narrow room with a lowish ceiling and an entire wall of glass looking over the harbour. And the room was packed with 100 people dining (they'd sold out).

Our particular line-up that evening has been working as a team for years. We know each other's quirks and foibles, and we know the repertoire *backwards* (one day I'll learn it the right way around, but I always was different to other people). So, much of our rehearsal time is spent working out the staging and the acoustics of the room.

We will sing bits of the pieces, usually working from the end of the show backwards to prime the voices for the beginning. And we'll be checking for dynamic levels, sweet spots and dead areas, and delays. As well as the low ceiling and long room, for this performance the singers were literally in the middle of the audience and were going to have to do what we call a "Lighthouse gig" – revolve as they sing to include every member of the audience.

Also, our performing spaces were dotted around the room and were mostly made up of corridors between the tables, dodging around four pillars, and squeezing between the chairs to reach the next spot. Oh yes, and an exit through the fire doors during "O soave fanciulla" to sing the final high Cs on the balcony overlooking the harbour (and scaring the neighbours).

During the rehearsal we discovered a slight delay in the acoustics – the moment the singers went further than 8 feet from the piano, they were starting to sing behind the beat. In addition, there was no way they were going to be able to unleash the full power of their voices due to the size of the room and proximity of the audience. I still think people are quite thrilled and amazed at the power of an unamplified operatic voice – and most of the time our singers aren't going full out!

So the order of the evening was:

- keep moving while you sing
- turn as much as possible to include everyone in the room
- rework the choreography while you're singing to make sure you don't hit anyone
- no "racking up" until the money notes
- be careful about singing towards the windows as the sound will bounce back
- sing ahead of the beat if you're more than 8 feet from the piano
- and of course, remember the words.

While all this sounds very complicated, we're used to doing it, and we had a great night. The audience loved what we did, and I got to wear the blond wig again. In fact, they liked it so much that they were standing at the reception afterwards trying to book seats for the next year's performance (and we hadn't even been booked!).

Next year, I'm going to arrive early and spend some downtime in the hotel's sumptuous spa. I wonder what the acoustics are like in the swimming pool?

* * *

## A TRAVELLING LIFE FOR ME…

I've spent the last 20+ years as a touring musician – five-monthly, weekly, daily, even four shows a day *in four different towns* (that was a blast).

My favourite singers to work for are the lovely Hatstand Opera. I've worked with Hatstand for over 20 years, so we know each other inside out. We've done expensive gigs at the Savoy in London where even the *flowers* cost £20,000. And we've done a gig (the previous night in fact) in a village hall ankle-deep in brick dust with three walls and a sheet of tarpaulin as the builders were in. Yes, that's genuine.

One of my favourite jobs with Hatstand was the annual tour of the Channel Islands. If you don't know them, they're a group of islands off the south coast of England – the main ones are Jersey, Guernsey, Alderney and Sark.

The tour is a whirlwind of organization and travel, with eight concerts in four days on four different islands. The order differs depending on the tides(!) but normally it's fly to Jersey, then a tiny plane to Alderney, back to Guernsey, boat to Sark and back and then home. Each island has its own character and audience, and each one is a total joy. The evening audience on Alderney is huge fun, always packed and up for anything. The schools concert on Sark is unique as there's one school with children ranging from 6 to 16 in one class. Contrast that with the Jersey schools concert of 250 kids gagging to be entertained. Then the wonderful Guernsey concert hall with one of my favourite ever pianos, a Steinway grand, and a sell-out audience.

The only time this tour went wrong was when we got stuck on Alderney due to fog, and the tiny 12-seater plane couldn't leave. We were on a 15-minute scramble alert for 3 days! In the end the boys had to get back so we climbed on the coastguard's fishing boat from Alderney to Guernsey (in a force 5 gale thank you very much), got the Catamaran from Guernsey to Weymouth, car to North London (thanks to our baritone's excellent and patient partner), tube and train back home. Twenty-six hours door to door.

Tired, moi?

* * *

## FALLING OFF A LOG

Back in 2002 I wrote a chapter for the *Successful Singing Auditions* book with Gillyanne on the FOAL Process. This is the process for finding your Falling Off A Log areas that I created to help you identify great song repertoire.

I have added a few more questions since the book was published, and now include a question on "what would you be cast as, in a non-speaking TV commercial?" This is a useful question as it relies on your look and your energy-type, rather than your voice or singing styles. For those of you who are interested (and those who know me), given my look and energy type I would be cast as a vicar, a university lecturer, a musician or a mad scientist (how true life is).

I run workshops on casting and repertoire, and on one occasion we identified the students as a wacky Human Resources manager, a Disney newlywed, a gas-station attendant with a dead body in a cupboard behind her, and the man left out of the group in a pub in Malaga.

Having got our FOAL words and commercial castings, I then took a song and worked it with different subtexts to fit the casting and the FOAL key phrases. I also introduced the students to an exercise I use a great deal in my private sessions as a singing coach – changing the subtext to fit different types of audition. So Sondheim's "Good Thing Going" became suitable not only for the original (Sondheim show ballad) but also for *Les Misérables* (grittier, more dramatic, darker, more heightened emotions) and for *Beauty and the Beast* (more lyrical, smoother, regretful, higher passions). It's a very effective way of making your audition portfolio work harder for you.

* * *

## NO, BELTING DOES NOT START ON THE A BELOW MIDDLE C

I had a new client today. A young, slim, woman in her early twenties who looks a lot younger. Typical of the build, she has a high soprano voice (lowest note A below middle C, sits comfortably up to E a tenth above, and then goes on up into the stratosphere.

Students from music college or dance college often carry odd memories with them. Part of my job as a vocal and performance coach is to find out what beliefs about singing the client has (see our Webinars "How We Diagnose": Parts one and two for full details of our diagnostic list).

### *What Is Your "Belting Range"?*

Today's singer had been told that, as a young high soprano, her belt voice would be from the A below middle C (A3) to the D a ninth above (D5), and that people just didn't belt any higher.

Sorry, but that's enough to make me spit right there.

NO-ONE belts at the A below middle C. Not even basses. This is a misunderstanding of what belt is.

I'm afraid it became obvious that this choice piece of misinformation came from a classically trained (and biased) teacher – the sort you find occasionally teaching in a musical theatre dance school and who doesn't see the need to use anything other than their old classical training.

What you end up with is a large bunch of confused graduands who are unprepared for the rigours of singing in musical theatre, and with totally unrealistic ideas of what their voice can or can't do.

Back to today's client. Because she'd been told that she must be belting at the middle F (F4), she was overweighting her voice and using some strange dark resonance to try to get more thickness to the sound. Result? A self-fulfilling prophecy. She had been told she couldn't belt above D5, so she couldn't.

Now I've worked with a lot of voices like this – clean, clear and bright. In this case the singer was very comfortable singing legit, with notes up into the stratosphere.

This type of singer tends to have a speech quality that is neater than a heavier voice, and without the punch. The speech quality will go quite happily to C, D or E5 a tenth above middle C without much effort. And if she can't do that, she's usually using too much fold mass, too big a resonating space or too low a tongue and larynx in an attempt to "push chest voice up".

So, 5 minutes into the lesson it became clear very quickly that this soprano's belt voice actually STARTS at the D a ninth above middle C and goes on up. Within minutes of being given exercises appropriate to her voice type, she was belting D5, and went on to belt the G5 (an octave and a half above middle C) without even realizing where she was.

The result was a much easier, more appropriate, more holistic sound that she felt she could sustain, and one she felt was more "her". Once she'd got over the shock!

### *Time to Lay It on the Line*

First, know your voice types. A small, bright, young soprano in her early twenties in a slim, small body is NOT going to be belting until AT LEAST the C above middle C if not higher.

Second, even if she's got amazing super Fs and can trill around at the top of the stave, she still needs to be able to sing much of her repertoire in a more contemporary vocal setup in the middle range for her casting. It's no use ignoring that and just working on the top notes. Again.

And one last thing. She's not going to be producing the thick dark sound of an Idina Menzel, so don't give her "Pirate Queen" or "Defying Gravity" to sing.

Even if you think she might look good in green.

To find out more about belting and range, check out our double DVD *Belting Explained!*

* * *

## MASTERCLASSES

I love doing masterclasses. It's a real art to be able to give each student something positive to work with that won't disturb their current learning situation too much, but that will move them on in their performing. And you need to educate and entertain the audience. And you need to do it in 15 minutes or less.

To pull that off successfully requires a great deal of knowledge at your fingertips, instant empathy with each student, and an ability to identify the single most important thing you can give in the simplest way possible, to leave time for the student to experiment.

I recently gave an online masterclass (I've always wanted my face up on a 60-foot screen) to a group of musical theatre students in a university at the other end of the country. And having worked with six of them on their songs in just under an hour, I really kicked it up a notch.

### *We Played "Speed Diagnostics"*

Each student sings 30 seconds of their second song (or their best 16 bars – see my other articles on this topic above). I give them an instant diagnosis of a technique or performance tip that will improve that piece, we try it out and I move on to the next student. All in 2 minutes or less. Six singers, six songs, six technical tips, in just over 10 minutes.

I've done this since in live masterclasses and it's a hoot. Everyone accepts this singing "speed dating", so the stakes are high but so is the energy. It's a great way to finish a masterclass.

* * *

## COLLABORATIVE PIANISTS UNITE

I've got various Google Alerts set up that tell me if there is anything interesting out there in internetland. The alert told me that my blog has been discovered by another pianist and blogger. Christopher Foley is Professor of Collaborative Piano and Chamber Music at the Royal Conservatory of Music Community School in Toronto. He's also the author of the excellent Collaborative Piano blog.

Collaborative piano is the new name across the pond for piano accompaniment. I rather like it. It sums up far more accurately the job of a pianist who works with other musicians. One thing an accompanist does NOT do is follow. Whatever music I am playing, whether it's opera, lieder, Victorian parlour song or musical theatre, I don't tag along with the singer, three steps behind with a bowed head. Accompaniment is essentially the art of working with people. In my experience, I take what someone gives me and work with it to improve, support, lead and co-create. This is also a feedback loop, in that whatever I do will cause the performing partner to react, improve, support lead and co-create in return. In a good duo or trio partnership this can lead to some extraordinary performances.

As a collaborative pianist (CP) both by training and by inclination, I have a certain bias. I think to be a CP you must have wide-ranging musical tastes and be flexible enough to accommodate and incorporate another's strong desires and decisions. Most CPs I know are excellent musicians who are (on the whole) extremely reliable and consistent. They are also usually nice people to know. But then I would say that. There is a fine article on Chris's site that lists the preferred skills for the collaborative pianist. It's a long list. And as someone who has worked in most branches of the music business, I can say that it's pretty accurate.

There is one more thing I would add – a strong sense of self-worth. It's one job where the better you are, the less people notice you. Sad but true. And one more thing – yes, I AM good enough to be a solo pianist. I simply prefer co-creating with other people to being locked in a room for 6 hours a day in front of a keyboard. Mind you, I've written a blog, a website, a handful of #1 bestselling books and eBooks, articles and reviews for magazines, scripts for vocal physiology videos…

Maybe I've just swapped one locked room with a keyboard for another…

* * *

## HOW MUCH DO YOU NEED TO KNOW?

Do you really need to know which muscles are moving in which direction in order to be able to sing?

First, it is of course perfectly possible to sing without any knowledge whatsoever – mothers do it all over the world with their babies. Singing in this instance is a communication and mirroring thing – leading your child's education or mirroring their feelings and thoughts. Taking this question into the realms of the profession needs a slightly different response.

The role of the professional singer is to create a performance at the highest level that (s)he is capable of, and to be able to sustain something approaching that level of performance repeatedly. This usually means that the singer has to know at least a little how the sound is made and reproduced. Of course, there are singers who just open their mouths and are blessed with a voice that works each time and that enables them to express whatever it is that they want to express in whatever circumstance they find themselves. If you are one of these singers, thank your lucky stars, then line yourself up with a good coach, a set of ears you can trust – you are living on a knife-edge.

The reason for that last comment? I haven't met a singer yet (with any longevity in their career) that hasn't had some problems with their voice or performance. I have also been witness to a number of "natural" singers who have found on leaving college that they have absolutely no idea how their voice works, and so have no defences when something goes wrong.

Both Gillyanne and I have worked with a number of these singers, helping them to rehabilitate themselves when the unthinkable happens. The "trick" (if there is one) is to give the minimum amount of technical input necessary, without either confusing or overwhelming. The purpose of a technique in any branch of the arts seems to be to act as a conduit for the expression of the artist. I have had a number of clients who have been worried that learning something about the technicalities of sound production will destroy their "gift" or their performing spontaneity. However, having enough technical knowledge gives a performer the real confidence to know what is going to happen when they open their mouth, which leads to more experimentation, more confidence and often to a higher level of artistry.

I have also had experience of teachers attempting to start from scratch with new students who are already performing professionally. While this is great for the teacher's ego, it does nothing for the client except cause more anguish and concern. The singers we work with usually have long-term commitments to shows or companies and find themselves having trouble in the middle of a run. They simply don't have the time (or money, or reputation) to put a hold on their contractual obligations.

Of course, this can mean that in the short term, quick fixes are often the order of the day. But in these circumstances each role will have its particular problems and quirks which needs specific answers. And the best quick fixes are based on a profound knowledge of physiology and its appropriate application.

In answer to the opening question, if you're a singer, no, you don't need to know what all your muscles are doing – you'd go insane if you tried! But if you are having problems with your singing (and who doesn't at some point in their lives) specific, technical and muscular input can revolutionize the way you understand the craft of performing.

And if you're a teacher – absolutely!

* * *

## HOW MUCH DO *THEY* NEED TO KNOW?

Following on from the previous article ("How much do you need to know") I had an interesting question from one of my readers in Israel.

> Hi Jeremy, your blog is very valuable and enjoyable for me. I often find it hard to teach people that are working already in the theatre or just need some "brush-up" on their technique. They want to come for very few lessons and get some "tips" from me.

This is an interesting challenge, and one I am familiar with. As a teacher, you have so much to give, and so many options to help clients get the best out of their voice and performance. But what happens when all they want (or feel they can afford) is one or two sessions? How do you deal with the time factor and the overwhelming desire to pass on what you know?

Well firstly, there's an old English saying: you can lead a horse to water, but you can't make it drink. Essentially, I can't force people to accept what I have to offer, if they don't want to know! What I think people require and what they think they require don't always coincide.

And since we're on the subject of old English sayings, the other one that comes to mind is "Why buy a dog and bark yourself?" If you are coming to a teacher to learn, it makes sense to listen to what they have to say, rather than insisting that you know how to fix any problems. However, if the client is there to seek advice (and to pay for it), and if they choose not to ask, listen or accept it, that is entirely their choice.

I work with clients from completely different backgrounds and professional levels, and it is fascinating to discover certain patterns.

My student clients are still in the process of learning and will often need fairly firm guidance and regular input. I will often set out a short "plan" at the beginning of the session to clarify what we are going to work on. This will often include technical information, performance information or anything that I feel the young client needs for a successful career. The focus here is on long-term training.

Once you step into the professional market, the requirements of a client are different. I will often get one-off drop-ins, who come for a brush-up before an important audition. These clients want advice, practical tips and above all, security, to know that what they are about to present to an audition panel is appropriate. Much of this session will be spent tweaking what the client already does.

The focus here is on short- to mid-term career sustaining. This is an interesting group, as I often get repeat visits from these clients who feel that I have helped them get further in the audition process and want more information from me. They can sense that I know a great deal more than I have told them, but that I have focused on their immediate needs, rather than forcing them to "change their technique".

There is one type of client in this category however who comes for "a singing lesson" the day before their audition, and who doesn't have the technical ability to sustain a song. More about that later.

The third category is the high-level performer, the leading man or lady or the well-known actor/actress. These performers will often be invited to audition for specific roles or shows and need confidence in their material and ability more than anything else. The focus here is building up what is already there, rather than giving new technical information. The only exception to this is when the singer is working a song that contains a particular technical challenge that really can be solved in 15 minutes (it happens more often than you would think). The focus here is on instant or short-term coaching.

Part of the problem stems from how one is viewed – as a technical teacher, a guru, a coach or a quick-fixer. In order to be of the most value to your clients, you have to listen to and judge what they need. And sometimes your satisfaction is not theirs!

Ultimately, in order to feel comfortable yourself, you must work with the person in front of you and pay attention to their requirements. The following two statements are odd, but true.

If you do what you think is a good job, you may not get a repeat booking.

If you do what they think is a good job, not only will you be likely to get a repeat booking from them, but you will probably get a glowing reference and more clients too.

And in the case of the clients who come for one session but who have an unrealistic idea of their singing voices? Find one thing to fix and fix it. Then let them go and hope that eventually they will realize that they need more lessons. If they do, you'll be the person they'll come back to.

* * *

## WHY IS SINGING SO SCARY?

Even when you get to the status of Martin Freeman, star of Hollywood films, the BBC smash hit *Sherlock*, and cult figure in *The Office*, singing holds a certain terror.

In his own words,

> It's improvised singing. It's not the world's great ambition to hear me sing, trust me. The world doesn't need that – it's got war. I'm hardly Aldershot's Sammy Davis.

Apparently, it even outweighs appearing naked on screen – Martin was the shy naked body double in the hit film *Love Actually*. In the film *Confetti*, Martin and *Spaced* star Jessica Stevenson had to learn a high-kicking, tap dancing MGM musical number for their wedding scene.

> I didn't find the dance-steps that easy to pick up either but, in the end, I loved doing it. I think most actors are show-offs and have at some point spent afternoons singing along to West Side Story. I'm big fan of musicals, but I hadn't been in one since drama school 10 years ago.

It took two years to edit down the 150 hours of material recorded for *Confetti* into a 100-minute film. And improvised singing is not the only difficult thing for "the new face of M&S menswear":

> I was asked to do a reading at a wedding and I couldn't do it. It was really embarrassing. It was impossible for me to get through without breaking down. It took me about 20 minutes to do and in the end one of my brothers had to get up and put his arm around my shoulder for moral support before I could do it. I'm sure everyone thought I was just another luvvie, auditioning for a role.

So, performance nerves and wedding speeches don't just paralyse the man next door. But why is singing (or giving speeches) so scary?

Singing first – I find that mostly it's because the performer doesn't feel that they know what they are doing. Perhaps singing is not a comfortable mode of expression, or perhaps they just don't know what to focus on. In my audition coaching I will often spend time with actors on the focus of the story, or the emotion that needs portraying. Or I will provide simple techniques that enable the actor to make the appropriate sounds.

In my performance coaching, I might work with speech-makers (or recently a PowerPoint presenter) on the purpose of the speech, the reason for you giving it, and offer hints and achievable goals on breathing, grounding and focus. And of course, to speak in the way that fits you, rather than how you think you SHOULD speak.

One recent (and very nervous) auditionee for a lead role in *Phantom* went into the final audition with several clear goals for each song. He was able to notice when his nerves were about to take over and was able to shift his focus to some of his personal goals. He came out satisfied that it was the best audition he could do that day. And you can't ask more than that!

*   *   *

## SINGING TEACHER OR VOCAL COACH?

What's the difference between a singing lesson and a vocal coaching session?

Is there a difference between a singing teacher and a vocal coach, and does it matter? Gillyanne and I are a singing teacher/vocal coach duo combination, and we have been team teaching for 20 years. We think there IS a difference, and that each are important to a singer's career.

### *The Singing Teacher*

The first difference between a singing lesson and a vocal coaching session is the focus of the lesson. Singing teachers work on vocal technique. You may do vocal function exercises, note patterns and single notes, designed to achieve a particular sound or to refine your ability in a particular part of your range. Typically, the majority of the lesson will be given to these technical exercises, although there may well be some time given to song troubleshooting – putting the technique into context. Sometimes you do not get to sing a song all the way through in a technique lesson, as the purpose is to discover the things that are not working for you, and to fix them.

The second difference concerns the structure of the lesson. A good singing teacher will be helping you build your vocal technique and stamina, so will give you structured homework, vocal exercise routines to practise, and will plan technical instructions over an extended timespan.

Many singing teachers will use a combination of technical information, gut feeling and performance or style coaching in their sessions. It's interesting that with all the people I've worked with and played for in the last 30 years, there have been only three true vocal technique teachers. These are teachers who understand vocal function on a very deep level, can listen to your voice, take it apart and give you precise technical input to improve it immediately, in one shot or lesson after lesson. The training we give on the Vocal Process Teacher Accreditation Programme guides singing teachers to exactly that – precise vocal diagnosis, a deep understanding of vocal function and physiology, and a creative flair for accurate, targeted exercises and routines.

### *Singing Teacher Negatives*

Be aware that there are unskilled singing teachers out there, who give the same exercises to every student regardless of the technical difficulty or the individual vocal makeup of the student. And if it doesn't work the first (second, fifth, twentieth…) week it's clearly "because you just aren't working hard enough at it".

A word about singing teachers and performance advice: when a singing teacher offers you advice on your performing, make sure that they are speaking from experience, and that they have worked in the genre they are talking about. Working as a singer in the opera field is very different from working in the contemporary musical theatre world, or on the cover band gig. Be prepared to take performance tips with a small pinch of salt unless it's the teacher's home ground.

### *The Vocal Coach*

The vocal coach will expect you to know how to sing and will help you put your technique into a context, find the best version of your voice and style for each song, and help you create, understand and polish your performing persona. It is likely that you will sing songs all the way through, as the purpose of the session is to discover how you perform, what you do with the song material and whether your view/concept works for you.

Vocal coaches can cover many things including musical style, phrasing, memorizing, acting or atmosphere intent, finding your version of the song, choosing music for a set, audition technique and even go as far as advice on your "look".

As with the singing teacher, the really skilled vocal coach can listen to you speak or sing and identify your strengths, help you find an authentic performance, and give you targeted, personalized performance techniques to help you find the best version for (and of) you. Many choral conductors are good vocal coaches, aiming to get the best performance from their groups.

### *Vocal Coach Negatives*

A word about vocal coaches and vocal technique advice: if your vocal coach starts giving you technical information like "you need to lower your larynx" or "you're not twanging hard enough", make sure they have formal training in vocal pedagogy and are qualified to give vocal technique advice. Many vocal coaches just pick up phrases and concepts as they go along and use them without knowledge of individual voices and the limits of each technique.

And just as you don't need any certificates to become a singing teacher (or indeed any knowledge or experience), there are no qualifications to become a vocal coach. Although many vocal coaches have worked at a high level in the music industry as performers (often on keyboards or as a conductor), not all of them have sung professionally. They are usually instrumentalists first, so will have a good grasp of music and style. There are a handful of vocal coaches who really know about the physiology of the voice so when you meet a coach who can do both, treasure them!

With either the singing teacher or the vocal coach, a wide knowledge base and a sense of context are vital. Gillyanne and I have not yet found the exercise that works for every singer in every context. If a teacher tells you that "this exercise works for everything", take a deep breath and run away.

### *The Industry*

Different branches of the professional singing industry seem to favour either the teacher or the coach for their singers.

The commercial recording industry appears to prefer vocal coaches (often music and style coaches, some of whom know next to nothing about vocal function) and will only call in singing teachers (if ever) in emergencies.

The classical music industry seems to prefer singing teachers to vocal coaches (who are usually accompanists first and foremost). That's certainly the way I started more than 30 years ago – I was an accompanist who started coaching in desperation at the repeated mistakes my singers were making in their understanding of music and performance. Then I studied vocal function to find out how the vocal instrument worked and what would cause them to sing like that!

Gillyanne and I have complementary skills and will often work with the same student, either consecutively or in the same lesson. This allows us to combine our strengths to give the singer the best possible support for their career. If you've never seen us team-teach, book a session with both of us or come to a masterclass – it's a powerful experience.

Ultimately, whether you go for someone with a technical knowledge base, a practical experience base or just a personality you like, you need to remember that YOU are responsible for looking after your voice – if it feels wrong, don't be persuaded that it's right for you.

And a final thought – whether you work with a singing teacher or a vocal coach, keep your personal bullshitometer on full alert!

Figure 6: The Vocal Process Bullshitometer™

You may have similar problems to those described in the book, or you may be struggling to move forwards with your singing. Or it may be that you're curious to find out what would happen to your voice and performing if I coached you personally. If so, book a session with me here:

https://DrGillyanneKayesJeremyFisherInspirationSession.as.me/JeremyCoaching

I'll see you soon.

# ABOUT JEREMY

## PIANO

Jeremy Fisher began piano lessons at 7 and finished at 7.30. He nearly gave up when his piano lessons clashed with *Mission Impossible* on TV.

He has performed in every imaginable venue, including a prison, in the display window of a shopping centre, and 150 feet underground in a pothole.

He studied oboe, piano and accompaniment at the RNCM and won a national collaborative pianist prize at the age of 21. He was guest solo artiste for the Yamaha Corporation for 5 years.

As a West End musician since 1988, Jeremy has worked on many shows including *Les Misérables*, *Phantom of the Opera*, *Me and My Girl*, *A Chorus Line* and *Carmen Jones*. Jeremy's 2002 book *Successful Singing Auditions* with Dr Gillyanne Kayes was based on his experience of more than 8,500 auditions in London's West End.

## VOICE

Jeremy is also a singing voice specialist and has worked as a repetiteur for four Opera companies. He has written many books on singing including *Successful Singing Auditions* (2002), the *Singing Express* series for children (2009-11), *This Is A Voice* (hardback 2016, paperback 2018) and a chapter on "Pedagogy in Different Sung Genres" in *The Oxford Handbook of Singing* (2019).

In 2018, Jeremy's ebooks *How To Sing Legato* and *How to Accompany your Singing Students* both became Amazon #1 bestsellers on their first day.

The Science Museum in London commissioned Jeremy to create a "Voicebox Video" showing the inside of a singing larynx. His work has been featured on the BBC's science programmes *Leading Edge* and *Science In Action*, broadcast worldwide to more than 44 million people. The One Minute Voice WarmUp App has already reached #1 on Google Play and #3 on the Appstore.

Jeremy has presented on singing and performance techniques in the UK, Spain, Sweden, Latvia, the Netherlands, the US and Australasia. He has lectured in Musical Theatre at RCSSD, Royal Conservatoire of Scotland and Guildhall School of Music and Drama. His vocal folds have featured on the British Voice Association leaflets and have appeared on Channel 4 as an example of a healthy voice. He works with musical theatre performers, actors, songwriters, classical singers and on repertoire, style, performance integration and career planning.

In his spare time, Jeremy sleeps and eats.

## POSTLUDE

Thank you for getting this far.

It's been a pleasure writing these articles, blogs and thoughts. I hope you've enjoyed climbing inside the mind of a vocal coach. If you have, please give the book (and me) an honest review and let your friends and singing colleagues know about it.

To finish, here's an article I wrote recently that is somewhat different to my usual style. Music is an extraordinary vibrational form that can cross physical boundaries and borders – I felt that this viewpoint was worth expressing.

* * *

## GOOD VIBRATIONS – DISCOVERING YOUR OWN SPECIAL "TUNE"

Think of the sound of a ruler on the end of a desk, a guitar string or a pair of vocal cords. When something vibrates at a regular speed, the human ear senses the vibrations as sound, specifically pitched sound. But go beyond the sense of hearing. There is a school of thought that states that all matter is vibration.

Think of everything in the world being a vibration. Consider whatever we do as having a vibration. Think of actions as being vibrations, and the result of our actions having vibrations that spread through our world, impacting on things and people around us. Go one stage further and think of the world as being the embodiment of all our vibrations, the result of our actions. We are sending out vibrations every second of every day – consciously or unconsciously. There is nothing new in this thought – world religions have talked for centuries about cause and effect, "do as you would be done by", "what goes around comes around". It is a small leap of imagination to think of these vibrations as being "in-tune" or "out-of-tune". But what does that mean?

When we are "in-tune", the vibrations we send out are clear, pure, definite and have potential for growth, an inspirational life of their own. The ripples that spread outwards from those original clear, pure and definite vibrations have impact – sometimes a great impact – on the people who touch our lives.

When we are "out-of-tune", the vibrations we send out are muddy, confused, clouded, and have a potential for destruction and disharmony, for a removal of power and energy. These vibrations can be in the realm of sound – the words we speak, the tone of voice we use, the emotions we communicate. They can be in the realm of vision – the face we present to the world, the colours and clothes we choose to represent our selves. They can be in our attitudes – the conscious and unconscious ways we react to and interact with people, places, objects and ideas.

### *Discovering Your Own Special "Tune"*

To discover your own "tune", you might begin by looking at your powerful emotions, in the extreme situations, in your automatic responses. When you suddenly realize that you won't stand for that unfair situation, when you don't act in the same way as your peers, when you are prepared to lose your job because of a strongly held principle. These are the times when your "tune" creeps up on you and steps out into the public eye to make sure you follow your beliefs. Then you can recognize these moments and "tune-in" to the more subtle signs – the gut feelings, the nagging little worries, the second thoughts. The things that go against your self but that speak softly, that can be easily overlooked.

When you have tuned in to those, you can then begin to notice the blemishes, the "accidentals", the melodic eddies in your song – are they what you want to express or are they leading you away from your self? Is this the best expression of you that you are able to perform? You can begin to decide what your tune is and what changes you wish to make – your melody becomes conscious and you join with its creation.

But does being "in-tune" mean being in accord with everyone or everything around us. Is there room for different tunes or should we all be singing from the same hymn-sheet? Sometimes, when we are "in-tune" with ourselves, the ripples we create can move against the current, stand apart from the prevailing climate, cause outrage. Perhaps those ripples disturb something that has been accepted as the status quo, something that may no longer be relevant. Or perhaps those ripples appeal to a group of people different from the group you currently inhabit. It may be time for a change… If you are genuinely in-tune with yourself and your own truth, it is the most important thing in the world. You will behave in a way that is consonant with your truth. And that behaviour will have power, simply by its own resonance with itself.

So your tune – your melody – may NOT immediately coincide with the world around you. It may cause discomfort for the people around you. It may invite their aggression or their pity or their dismissal. But if it is consonant with your own highest truth, it will be ultimately good for you to express it. And your tune will attract others who appreciate and mirror it, people with whom you can create harmonies, chorales. This attraction works for any level of understanding and growth – junkies can attract junkies or those who support them, and when a junkie changes their tune (their personal beliefs and resonances), those supporters of their previous life melt away to be replaced with supporters of their new beliefs and expressions.

Possibly only a few people will understand your particular resonance – but you will be greater and happier and more at peace through expressing it.

Not everyone will like your tune, not everyone will appreciate your particular melody. Your melody, once expressed, may temporarily attract those who dislike it intensely and who seek to change it. For this is a world of contrast, and a melody can only exist and be recognized against a background of countermelody and distortion. Only by having something to decide against can we decide consciously to move towards something else.

After all, if we all liked the same music, there would be no new music, no surprises, no creation, and ultimately no respite. Ultimately, the vibrational strength and purity of your personal melody can give others the reason to express their own melody. And the purer and more conscious your melody is, the easier it is for different melodies to fit together.

Since everyone and everything vibrates, imagine the experience of all those melodies harmonizing together. Consider a world where individuals are designed to resonate individually, and once they are singing their own "tune", whatever their tune is, the individual resonances build into a world-beating harmony. The world will literally be shaken to the core by the combined vibrations of the people on it. Because only when you express and embody what you think you are, will the world become an easier, more joyous, more fun place to live in.

* * *